COMPILED BY
ANNIE GIBBINS

Copyright © 2023 by **Annie Gibbins**

All rights reserved. No part of this book may be used or reproduced by any means, graphic, electronic, or mechanical, including photocopying, recording, taping or by any information storage retrieval system without the written permission of the copyright owner except in the case of brief quotations embodied in critical articles and reviews. Because of the dynamic nature of the Internet, any web addresses or links contained in this book may have changed since publication and may no longer be valid. The views expressed in this work are solely those of the author and do not necessarily reflect the views of the publisher and the publisher hereby disclaims any responsibility for them.

Annie Gibbins/Women's Biz Publishing
New South Wales, Australia
www.womensbizpublishing.com

Book Layout © 2023 womensbizpublishing.com

Heart Warrior/ Annie Gibbins -- 1st ed.
978-1-922969-01-9

womensbizglobal.com

Contents

LUMBIE MLAMBO 1
ANNIE GIBBINS 5
ALLY HENSLEY 14
KAREN P WEAVER 20
HELEN GLEN 28
PEIMING SUN 41
SHARON LYNNE 49
PATRICIA JO GROVER 57
KELLY MARKEY 63
DR LAURA COBB 73
DR TALAT UPPAL 83
ANNIE GIBBINS 91

COMPILED BY ANNIE GIBBINS

FOREWORD

LUMBIE MLAMBO

When Annie Gibbins, a lifelong acquaintance, thought it appropriate for me to write this foreword, I was beyond elated. I've always loved giving back, and through my non-profit organisation, I've been blessed to help raise the status of women and girls around the world. I can sincerely say that following my heart has always been my guiding principle. My heart never lies to me. This trust enables me to lead with assurance and bring about major change. I've always allowed my fear to be overcome by my zeal for what I want.

Annie's book is a great compilation of the experiences of purpose-driven women. Undoubtedly, it will guide you on your path to achieving the seemingly impossible. For me, terrible incidents shaped my development into a strong-voiced humanitarian. While visiting my father, who was sick at the time, I suffered a stroke that left me partially paralysed. Shortly after that, my father passed away. He was revered in the community for his humanitarian work, and I committed to fulfil his promise and continue his unfinished work to improve a community clinic in Igusi, Zimbabwe.

I had no idea how much this endeavour would impact my life and help me in finding my own purpose. I observed an unmet need and a gap in the community that I could identify with. Lack of access to clean water prevents women and girls from economic opportunities granted as a human right to all. Since women and girls are typically responsible for collecting water, they spend almost the entire day doing so.

As a result, lack of time prevents them from attaining skills necessary to advance in life. Girls frequently miss school and significantly lag behind in their academics. Despite how difficult it may seem; this issue rose to the top of my list of priorities.

The stories in this book are quite relatable to me.

Annie's selection of tales of personal and professional struggles faced by women, show how they overcome their adversities and challenges, to become 'Heart Warriors'. The devastating incidents I experienced gave me the courage to channel my inner warrior to bring about the change I want to see in the world, rather than allowing my tragedy to prevent me from living my life. My main objective has always been inclusion of women at all levels. The value of what women contribute to the world economy is generally overlooked. So, in memory of my father, I established a non-profit organisation to promote inclusion, health and development, by facilitating marginalised communities' access to basic necessities like clean water, sanitary conditions and hygienic practices. This helps to combat poverty and advance gender equality. By trusting my inner voice, this is how I solve the issues faced by women and girls globally.

Annie helps us to see that women are not afraid to push the envelope. A strong woman is prepared to face difficulties, because doing so will fuel her strength for the future. We frequently overlook the fact that each of us is born a warrior. In line with Annie's push for strong women, is the need to have self-assurance and take pride in all of our accomplishments, no matter how small. Milestones don't just include the struggles to get there, but also the transformation of your perspective of the world around you, as your inner warrior guides you. When you start to completely appreciate your worth and value, you can then live a purposeful life.

Limitations, though flaws, do not characterise us. The real you—a strong, exceptional woman—is revealed when you tap into your inner warrior. You will stand up for what you believe in and defend fundamentally feminine principles as a woman warrior. For me, organising humanitarian initiatives and acting as a guardian of vital natural resources, allows me to express my inner warrior. Whatever my position, I can attest that I excel by championing change and motivating people along the way. My seemingly small actions have a significant impact on the local communities. Regardless of how a milestone turns out, I celebrate it and continue to define success as it pertains to myself. Failure doesn't deter me; instead, it fuels my curiosity, resiliency and the urge to innovate, create and learn from my experiences. Resilience, in the words of my mentor Tony O. Elumelu, is "That fiery drive that pushes you to never give up."

The Heart Warrior book is an excellent read, full of brave and inspiring tales told by strong women. So, release your inner strength and cultivate your firmly held beliefs about yourself, other people, and the world at large. Stories build people. Use your inner strength to leverage the powerful story that only you own. You are at your finest when telling your story, which only you are capable of doing. There is no such thing as a small story because only you, the owner, have a thorough understanding of it and the skills necessary to quantify it. Your story is unique to you, originates from your heart, and portrays the tenacious warrior inside you.

This book equips women for success and guides them to overcome obstacles that seem insurmountable in order to become independent. Heart Warriors keep defining what success means to them. I encourage you to continue listening to your inner voice and inspiring the change you want to see. The world needs to hear and feel the heartbeat of warriors like yourself, who choose to rise up and make the world a better plac

COMPILED BY ANNIE GIBBINS

THE HEART WARRIOR WITHIN

ANNIE GIBBINS

Doesn't it ultimately start with love?

Tonight, as I write this, I am sitting on my verandah, which is perfectly wrapped around my Australian sandstone house. I am sipping on my favourite white wine, nibbling on uneven chunks of blue cheese, and smiling quietly to myself. The noise of laughter, happiness and giggles from my granddaughter means it is anything but quiet, but I wouldn't want it any other way. As the summer sun bounces off the serene gum-trees, kookaburras sing their sunset song. The air is salty from the nearby ocean, and dew on the grass starts to appear, the signs of relief after a scorching Sunday in Sydney. I am staring at my family- my children, my grandchildren, and my one true love, James, my forever husband.

It's in this perfect instance that I realised, that this book of stories must be told. Not just by my lone voice, but from all those who have felt a love like this. Who have built their families, communities, and life's purpose from one single ingredient: Love. However, with love comes loss. With birth comes grief. With courage comes vulnerability. With power comes humility. This postcard image, that I am describing to you, wasn't just magically created. I didn't look longingly into the stars one night and plead with the Universe to deliver me a perfect life.

Sadly, creating the life you want is not that easy. However, what is easy, is identifying the heart you want to lead with. Is it courageous? Is it tenacious? Is it quietly stoic?

I hope reading this book gives you an insight into what it means to be a 'Heart Warrior' and leads you on the journey to discovering what kind of 'Heart Warrior' you are.

Love requires a heart that can break.

If we are lucky enough, we will all experience earth rattling love, at least once in our lifetime. A kind of love that is usually only reserved for movies. A kind of love where we go on the perfect date and immediately find our person. The kind of love that floods a body. The kind of love that makes us feel like the luckiest person on the planet. Sometimes, love can be made to look impossibly romantic. You know, the type we see in a vintage Parisian film, or a social media post, where the couple are looking longingly into each other's eyes over a Martini.

I'm not saying this 'ideal' portrayal of love is negative, on the contrary, it forces us to set our expectations beyond our limits. However, I think when we idolise love and put it on a pedestal as the 'be all and end all,' rather than thinking about ourselves, then that can have damaging consequences. It's an old cliché saying, 'In order to love someone else, you must love yourself first'. I hate to be the bearer of bad news, but cliches are cliches for a reason, because they are true.

You will never experience the full force of love, without some degree of loss. It's a brutal realisation, but love is the highest currency on this planet. It cannot be taken for granted, nor be toyed with. Without the risk of sounding too maudlin, this is an uplifting book after all, to be a warrior, you need to have fought and lost at some stage of your life. A Heart Warrior has seen their fair share of battlefields and by no means have they come out of the rough and tumble unscathed. Not everyone understands the motives of a Heart Warrior, be it their ambition to create the perfect family, relationship, or purpose. Perhaps, as a Heart Warrior, you have relentlessly tried to convince people as to why you have fought so hard. You always try to do what's best, and sometimes, you don't always get it right. Regardless, you take pride in the people you love, and you demand trust and respect in return.

When it comes to love, a Heart Warrior never hesitates. They run full pelt onto the battlefield and claim what they believe has been theirs all along. You too can be a Heart Warrior and lay claim to what you deserve, particularly when it comes to all matters concerning love.

Dare to be different!

In a world where comparison is the norm, measuring ourselves against our peers or loved ones is unavoidable. Whether you are attending a family lunch, a corporate dinner, or a community event, it's almost impossible not to put yourself up against others. However, when we use our comparative nature as a self-criticism tool, rather than an empowering one, we set ourselves up with a one-way battle of negative self-doubt and dangerous thoughts. See, for millions of years, we have floated in tribes. We sat in circles and shared stories. Over time, these have simply modernised into mother's groups, bible study classes, or creative meetups. It's so natural to sit with those we relate to the most. So, when does relatability turn to envy? When we dare to be different without apology or excuses.

Either consciously or subconsciously, adopting the validation of others is extremely important. Have you ever sat around for an evening meal with your extended family, for a relative to shout across the table, "So, when are you getting married? Why haven't you had children yet? Why haven't you been promoted yet?" Or worse still, "Why, when you're a mother, do you need to work in the first place?" These are the moments where you'd like nothing more than the ground to open up and swallow you whole, as for some reason, justifying your dreams has become everyone else's business.

I want to tell you what I think you should do instead, that is, design and live the life that feels right for you. In fact, better than right, perfect. Courage is often associated with habits that take grit to overcome, like leaving a relationship that wasn't right for you, or quitting a job because it filled you with dread. However, courage also comes in forms that are unrecognised, such as studying alone until the early hours of the morning, while my children sleep, to better my career and my family's future. Regardless of how your courage is demonstrated or pursued, being vulnerable to your dreams and desires takes some of the greatest courage you can muster, and it is this boldness which is at the core of every Heart Warrior.

You take the arrow for people who matter.

Gosh, if you can't tell, I am passionate about this subject. When I was a young mum to two sets of twins born just 26 months apart, and our beautiful daughter, who arrived five years later, people would always tell me to want 'less'. Not because they didn't believe in me (well, not everyone), but because they couldn't comprehend how I could possibly want to apply for a job as a CEO, that on paper, I wasn't completely qualified to have. However, much to people's chagrin, I am motivated by being told that I 'Can't' do something."

So, that's what I did. By day, I was a working mum alongside my supportive husband, James, who would tag-team school drop-offs, pickups, meals, and bath times. Then, despite my exhausted body craving nothing more than bed, I would then open my textbooks to study, until the early hours of morning, knowing that in just a few hours' time, my babies would wake hungry and in need of love.

Throughout this time, I made a pact with myself. I said, "Annie, don't negotiate with your life. You can do anything, and I mean, anything". Did I take an arrow for my family? Maybe. Did my body want to crash multiple times during those long, lonely hours poring over my textbooks? A little. But during my CEO career, I have always been aware of what counts and matters most. Now, when I look at my team, my friends, charity board members, clients, and most recently, the Women's Biz Global community, taking an arrow doesn't always mean to shield another from getting wounded. It means 'showing up'.

Throughout my career, I have witnessed many times where the 'underdog' is on the outside. Their ambition and ability may appear to be thriving, but their voice is quiet and timid. It's not that people aren't capable of rising to the challenge, they simply need shoulders to stand on. I have made it a goal of mine to celebrate, encourage and be the 'forever shoulders' for all those who deserve a spot in the limelight.

It's imperative as Heart Warriors, to prioritise any action or motive with integrity, love, and a determination to never leave anyone behind. Whether you are financially bailing out a family member, breaking down walls to fight for those who are hurt, or affirming your boundaries in the workplace, take the arrow firmly and point in the direction you want it to land.

Sometimes, you've just got to say no!

OK, so one of my all-time favourite topics is boundaries and how we can't and won't ever live without them. I cannot stress this enough; boundaries are the greatest gift we can give to ourselves and others.

Over the years, the topic of boundaries has had a bad rap. Boundaries have been seen as obstacles, preventions, barricades, and reasons to not do the right thing. Why? Because boundaries feel really difficult to enforce.

You know the early stages of a relationship, where you are head over heels for the other? You couldn't imagine that person ever disrespecting or misunderstanding you? Until they do. Not to say that every new romantic relationship is set to get harder. In fact, I am a sucker for a love story, because essentially, I am in one. However, my marriage to my childhood sweetheart has taken work, and our successful love is funnily enough, widely attributed to boundaries.

Think of boundaries as a set of permissions; an invisible fence between what is right for you and what simply won't work. You don't have to deliver a boundary contract of sorts, with hard and fast rules, however, if you don't put your invisible fence around your worth and self-respect, your boundaries may be ignored, unseen, or cause issues along the way.

In many ways, a Heart Warrior is unafraid to make hard decisions, or take a risk on love. If your boundary caused a lover to drift, they didn't deserve prime real estate in your heart in the first place. Perhaps you're the one who calls out the bad behaviour of a friend, colleague, or family member. Perhaps you need to be blunt and rock the boat a little, testing the boundaries of what is and isn't acceptable. Of course, we preface our actions as always coming from a good place, but ultimately, you do what you know is right and in doing so, the boundaries, or lack thereof, will speak for themselves.

Hear me roar!

It goes without saying that as a leader for women's empowerment, I have to touch on the topic of equality and equity. However, this book is not a vehicle to deliver my political opinion, instead, I want it to trigger change. Throughout my career, I have been the gender minority in a boardroom or at a conference event. I used to scan convention centre lobbies at post event receptions, thinking, "Where are all the women?" Fortunately, I can say that I have always been treated with respect, albeit the odd debasing comment from time to time. In many ways, my experiences have been relatable enough to speak about, but at times, damaging enough to silence me. However, I know that this is not the same for all women in my position and that is why I believe that we can and must do more. From time to time, I have spoken to friends and colleagues who haven't had it as easy, and THIS really irks me.

However, as a global Success Catalyst for all women and girls, I understand the importance of needing to lead with conviction and grace. We need to not fight anger with anger, but instead, take it head on with our intelligence, humility, emotional entourage, gusto, diversity, intrigue, capacity and tenacity.

As Heart Warriors, it is our contractual right to fight for what's right with moral obligation. We will roar with authenticity and be humble with silence. However, we must, and I mean absolutely must, speak the truth. And lastly, for those without a voice, we will speak their truth for them.

The truth won't stay quiet forever.

The truth is a funny thing. I don't mean truth, as in, truth versus lie. Sometimes, the truth is merely a standalone entity For example, have you ever sat in a work meeting and conjured up an excellent or insightful question or comment that is really valid, only to then hear your colleague ask it moments before you did? It's happened to me countless times and I'm often left kicking myself (metaphorically) and wishing I'd had the courage to speak up first.

Or perhaps you've had a fight with your partner, and instead of saying, "My needs aren't being met", one year down the line the same thing is happening, and you're left wishing you'd spoken up earlier. These are just some examples of everyday matters that silence us and prevent us from speaking OUR truth. Nearly a year ago, I quit my corporate gig to focus entirely on my business. I knew it would be a gamble. Although I had the business plan and roadmap of my idea carefully laid out, I knew that I would still have to back my brand and my truth to make it work.

Sometimes, I have to accept the fact my initial plan didn't go at all as I thought it would. Instead of being a smooth transition from one career to the next, I've had to learn technology, systems, protocols and move at a million miles per hour (my regular pace, for the record).

However, despite all these obstacles and challenges, I have continued to back my truth, and at the end of the day, I believe I deserve it.

The bottom line is: You deserve it all.
If no-one has said that to you, I will say it again: You deserve it ALL.

I am being direct with you, because as a Heart Warrior myself, the truth won't stay quiet forever. When you have that niggling desire to launch a podcast, create a business, or simply take up an activity that you've always wanted to do, don't wait a second more, because this is your truth.

Sometimes, the truth is a little more literal. We've all been there, where our friends seek counsel from us, about a cheating boyfriend, a cut-throat boss, or a situation that is causing them pain. But, more often than not, they make excuses for these behaviours and end up staying in toxic relationships or unfavourable situations. We never want to see the people we love suffer, but at the same time, we also need to deliver the truth. It hurts, like really hurts. However, what hurts more than delivering raw honesty, is the consequence of not doing so.

I ask you to deliver on your word, because that is the ultimate act of a spirited Heart Warrior.

Bring it on!

I ask you to deliver on your word, because that is the ultimate act of a spirited Heart Warrior.

I am a passionate hiker. In fact, if you're roaming the northern beaches of NSW, or find yourself climbing the mountainous peaks of New Zealand, you'll likely spot me, hoisting myself up the side of a mountain – recording voice-notes and closing business deals as I make my way up the summit.

Some might say, "I am trying to do it all", and do you know what? They are absolutely right. I am trying to do it all and I will never apologise for this ambitious streak of mine that I never plan to tame. As women, relentless pursuits are the makings of a happy human. Sure, it's not easy, and compromise is key, however, only when we truly band together, can we rise. Not as a solo adventurer, nor as a lone entrepreneur without supportive mentors, because to survive and thrive, we need our tribes.

I don't have to meet you to know that you picked up this book, because you are craving more. Remember the saying, "Looking for a sign, is a sign". Well, let this paragraph be your sign.

I know that you're a fighter, someone who has overcome trials, obstacles, loss and heartbreak. I know that you've sat in the dark, alone and unsure. I know that you've tried, and tried and tried, but you're just not getting that big break. I know that you have a lion spirit, but that it is struggling to roar. But I also know that you are steeped in hope, built from steel and laced with a desire for more. No matter what, you find the strength to keep going. You find the strength to open your heart.

Remember, a Heart Warrior loves boundlessly, dares to be different, will take an arrow, roars the truth and is an open fighter, one who will always act with kindness, compassion, and of course, fearlessness.

GRIEVING WOMANHOOD AS A CHILD

ALLY HENSLEY

So, my story goes a little something like this.

I will never forget the day the doctor pulled the curtain around my bed, opened my hospital file, and explained I was born with a unique condition called Mayer-Rokitansky-Küster-Hauser (MRKH) Syndrome. This life-altering condition affects one in 5000 females worldwide and is defined by the underdevelopment or absence of the uterus, cervix, and vaginal canal. I was in hospital because at 16 years of age, I'd never had a period, and to this day, I still haven't. Growing up, I was taught how a woman's body develops. I was taught that all bodies are the same. I was taught that women bleed and have babies. I was taught that a 'normal' body will go through certain changes and once this happens, "Congratulations, you've become a woman".

I am not a fan of the word 'normal'.

What I was not taught at school was that bodies can be different, and that I would never experience something so common, as a period. Following my diagnosis, everything I thought I knew about bodies unraveled in an instant.

Before being diagnosed with MRKH, like most teenagers rattling around the confusion of adolescence, I too was poised for this rite of passage to womanhood. At the time of learning I had MRKH, I had just celebrated my sweet sixteenth birthday. Instead of a celebration, I was learning that I would never be able to carry a child, long before I had even contemplated motherhood. I was learning that my vagina would need to be created from scratch. I was learning that womanhood for me was going to be a complex, intricate, and a beautiful collection of moving pieces, beyond just the physical.

As the doctor and nurse, also visibly stunned at my diagnosis, explained the treatment options, all I remember hearing was white noise and felt suffocated by the air, which was thick with the sickly smog of trauma. Sitting in the sterile hospital ward, my mum held my hand, as we both attempted to absorb the news. Her expression was akin to mine – stunned, afraid and confused. Hospital consultations can be brief at the best of times and before I'd even had a chance to gasp for some kind of answer, the doctor and nurse had moved onto their next patient.

Once the initial shock had set in, it was later explained to me that I was infertile and that to create a 'vagina', I would have to go to a London hospital to 'make one.'

"Is this really happening?", I thought.

With a bag big enough to fit three nights' worth of clothes in, I set off for London. Throughout this life-changing period, pardon the pun, my family was my emotional anchorage. Afterall, MRKH is a family diagnosis.
Parents, siblings, and partners do not go unfazed in this overwhelming process. However, we — my family and I — collectively banded together and headed off to the hospital. It was there where I commenced vaginal dilation; a lengthening technique using different size cylinders,

inserted into the entrance of my vagina 'dimple' (the pin-sized entrance that had never quite finished forming).

In case you're wondering, I do have a vulva and externally, you'd never know anything was different. I completed this process 'successfully' nine months later. I would be upstairs inserting cylinders into my body, a painful and intrusive act, while my family was downstairs desperately pretending, I wasn't.

The reason people with MRKH opt to pursue treatment may vary, assuming they are privileged enough to choose for themselves at all. For some, taking control in a powerless situation feeds the unknown. For others, it's about completeness, confidence, and of course, the pursuit of having a penetrative sexual relationship.

The emotional impact a person will feel, despite their choices to complete treatment or not, has the almighty power to send a woman into a devastating spin. It's hard to explain but MRKH is such a sensitive, complex condition that is layered with shame, identity, fertility-loss, hope, societal expectations and belonging.

Or in my case, un-belonging.

Even now, recalling the first years after being diagnosed renders me numb. I never felt 'enough'. I felt defected and apologetic for not being 'complete.' I would be grateful for bad relationships because I felt lucky enough just to be in one. I would lie in social circles about contraception, as I memorised the various brand names of contraceptive pills, so I wouldn't appear to be, 'not-quite-woman'.

But my life was not to live like this forever.

In my early thirties, I decided I no longer wanted to be a passenger, waiting for the universe to refund me a debt that was simply not owed. Taking accountability for happiness and acceptance often takes a series of turn-around moments. I needed to shed my victim status and start taking true responsibility for my happiness – whatever that looked like. When you are dealt with a game-changing reality, it takes immense inner strength to believe that there can be a promising future. Regarding childlessness, I am often asked in media interviews, "So Ally, how do you deal with infertility grief?"

And, the truth is, there is no one right answer.
Ah, grief, "hello".
Phew… here goes.

What I know is that healing isn't linear. Healing isn't neat, nor predictable. It's very messy and inconvenient. The infertility stigma fits into the box of 'complex grief.' It is both multi-faceted and brutal. We grieve for a child that isn't even born yet, we grieve a role we'll never play, we grieve an experience we'll never have. We grieve an expectation of what we thought womanhood may look like. We grieve a future that we need to recreate and replace with another. We grieve for our parents when we don't deliver a grandchild. We grieve a life that is suddenly spacious. We grieve a lost identity, as infertility constantly challenges our sexual identity and worth. We may even grieve again if we choose to visit motherhood later in life. We grieve so often that we forget what started our grieving in the first place. I don't know if we can, or are meant to, overcome grief, but I do know we are designed to get through it. Together, we will look it in the eye, acknowledge the pain it has caused us and say, "today grief, you are not mine'.

And only then will it seem less painful, less confusing.
With time, space, and hope, we will discover that womanhood is brave, unrelenting, and bold.

That our motherly love will redirect itself to those who need it.

Only then does grief not become our worst day, but our greatest asset in living a fulfilled and kick-ass life. Four years ago, I closed the chapter on becoming a mum (well, almost, but that story is in the book). On the 8th of January 2018, I left my IVF Australia appointment for the very last time. Just moments before, I had kissed my pregnant best friend, who'd been my rock throughout the whole process, goodbye and called my mum to ask her what I should do.

Although I already knew the answer, she confirmed it, "Ally, only you can answer this question".

I had the money in the bank, a surrogate on stand-by, and a baby-making folder with every blood test, ultrasound image, and hormonal test taken, neatly filed in alphabetical order. Right then and there though, I realised I wanted so much more than 'just' a baby.

I wanted a family.
But I didn't want to do it alone.
I didn't want to file transaction receipts, sperm donor guides, and excel spreadsheets anymore.
I wanted a father to be by my side.
I wanted to feel the first kick.

I sat there for a long time. It was possibly one of the loneliest moments of my life, but infertility is a lonely journey, especially for those of us who don't choose it.

But and there is always a but, motherhood truly does come in many different forms. Being known as 'Aunty Ally' to so many is just perfect for me. Families have opened their homes to me, and I have been humbled to give baths, read stories, settle tears and most recently, kiss the forehead of my newest nephew.

And, because there's always an 'and', it's okay to want a different ending. It's okay to grieve longer than someone else does. It's okay to miss your 'baby folder'. It's okay to never give up, whatever that looks like for you. And I guess, to be a 'Heart Warrior' means sometimes, you must take a piece of your own advice.

Two weeks ago, I gave an interview for a huge platform that was guaranteed to boost my profile. That's the goal for any new author, isn't it? I slapped on my make-up, reviewed the interview questions, and blasted myself with light-rings from every direction. The problem was, when I finished the interview, I realised that I didn't share the story the way I needed it to be, the way that honoured my backstory and the intricacies of my life altering MRKH diagnosis at 16 years of age.

So, I pulled it and took a gamble. I haven't looked back since.

But now I am free.

It's OK to want a different ending. It's OK to grieve longer than someone else does. It's OK to still miss your 'baby folder'. And it's OK if you never give up trying, whatever that looks like for you. There is always a different and happier ending, even when absolutely nothing goes to plan.

Never has society craved clarity more when it comes to societal norms, inclusivity, body ownership and LGBTI movements than now. With governments setting gender standards, unspoken infertility struggles on the downlow, and a rise in equality narratives – we can and must do more.

PURPOSE DRIVEN PURSUIT

KAREN P WEAVER

As a Heart Warrior, I've learned that leading with the heart requires courage and the willingness to push boundaries and choose trust over certainty. When I found my purpose in 2010 through writing my first novel, 'The Visitor,' I realised the power of storytelling and how it can heal, educate and inspire others. I'm passionate about serving others and showing up authentically in my work, and I believe that being true to myself and my values is key to success.

I'm an ambitious person, who loves finding new ways to do things and doesn't always follow rulebooks, instead I embrace challenges and grow through them. Inspired leadership means standing alongside others and creating a sense of community, not hovering over them. It's important to protect your heart and your space by surrounding yourself with positive, like-minded people and setting boundaries with toxic individuals. At the end of the day, you are only responsible for yourself and how you react to things, so choose positivity and love in everything you do.

One of my main Heart Warrior stories begins in 2010, when I set an intention to write my first book. A book that led me to choose to go on the journey of building my own publishing empire. This decision was inspired by my own writing journey and the realisation of the power of stories to connect with people's hearts and minds. To make this happen,

I committed to investing $50 a week in the business and believed it would take 25 years to achieve my goal of building a million-dollar award-winning press. However, it only took seven years.

My journey was not just about money, it's also been driven by the passion for story, but I really want to emphasise that I am a big believer in the importance of good people receiving their worth because when good people have money, good things happen.

During my early entrepreneur days, I set intentions and being open to opportunities that aligned with my purpose. I wanted to go on an adventure and share it with anyone who wanted to join me. I started doing three things every day towards my goals, these three things were not premeditated, they would come to me throughout the day, and I honoured them by gifting them the energy they needed by taking action. I began to trust that the universe would bring what I needed when I needed it, whether it was money, motivation, or other resources. I also learned to say "hell yes" to things that aligned with my intentions and 'hell no' to things that didn't.

I learned pretty early on that saying yes to something that my heart was a no to, was doing a disservice to that person, thing, event or whatever it was, as they would not get the best version of me. Instead, it would be done half-heartedly, no matter what my conscious efforts would be, my subconscious mind would wander back to my highest purpose.

If you are to learn anything from this chapter, I hope it is that a 'hell no' is as powerful as a 'hell yes'.

In 2015, when I went to my first 'Ausmumpreneur' conference, I realised that I had been playing it small, really small and I needed to start thinking bigger. And things led and inspired my thoughts, other things led me towards hiring a castle in Ireland and hosting a writer's retreat. It felt just like a natural next step for me. I was excited by it, loved the prospect of doing it and so thought, why not just do it? I did and it was worth it as we actually made a profit in the first year, which was amazing. Not a lot, but it counted for something. Although we brought in authors from all over the world and made amazing things happen, we certainly weren't making millions of dollars, even though people perceived us to be doing so.

Setting powerful intentions is one of the things that I have come to realise is really important, when you lead with the heart, you have to have courage, you have to push boundaries a little bit. And it doesn't matter if you have an ego or not. When you are led by the heart, you will do things out of your comfort zone, because you're on a mission. An example of this is that in the past, I would never have spoken out loud at conferences or public events, but when I found my purpose back in 2010, when I wrote my first novel, I learned that my story was of value to others and since then, I have spoken in front of hundreds of people, without succumbing to too many nerves. Driven by the knowledge that stories were powerful and that I was going to show up for my story.

Because when a story connects with someone, when they need to hear it, it will heal them, it will educate them, it will nurture them, it will make a difference in their life. It'll be a catalyst, as I believe that stories can inspire. I realised earlier on in life the power of story called upon me to be used as a vessel to share them. Since then, I've showed up with passion for service and with so much love, so much love for story.

Because I had moved from Ireland to Australia, one of the things I missed most was the sense of community. In Ireland, communities are valued and important. Whenever someone was at a low point or needed to learn something, it was always through a story. So, seeing the value in that, I showed up for it. To a community, it doesn't matter how a story is judged by others, it doesn't matter what the newspaper says, none of that matters at all. The only thing that matters is that stories are shared.

Once I started sharing stories myself, I ended up on this amazing journey that I could never have foreseen.

When I actually showed up for stories, something took over. Regardless of my other set intentions, the stories were more powerful than that. And I was open to the journey, a journey that came with the most amazing of experiences. One of the best things that I must share, and if you want to take anything out of my chapter, is that along the way, I did not have to compromise any of myself, or my values, for success.

I am an ambitious person. I'll be the first person to put my hand up to say that I love achieving things and I love finding new ways to do things. I don't tend to follow rule books, it's not in my DNA. Instead, I found a more efficient and fun way to do it.

I'm not a step taker to goals. As I said, I will go on the journey. I set intentions and set out to achieve them. And that comes with challenges and growth and all sorts of things. But I'm an 'embracer' of a challenge because I know that I'm evolving into the person who will be able to achieve my dreams.

Throughout this 'embracer' journey, I am inspiring others and showing them the way. I believe it's through my actions that I inspire others and, in this sense, being a Heart Warrior means being in the pursuit of my dreams, aligned with my purpose, and to serve well in that. And goodness, we're not perfect, like anyone, I've made mistakes, but I've never done anything ever to harm another.

I've only ever been of service and if ever I've fallen short for someone, I've gone out of my way to make sure that we catch up. I find it interesting to see how other people watch what I'm doing, observing and learning from me. I want to share my experiences with you and encourage you, as you begin your journey, to embrace the opportunities and make connections, as being authentic will be your biggest key to success.

Because I'm the same person when I'm speaking to the Duchess of York, when I'm speaking to my family, when I'm speaking to any of my authors, regardless of who I am talking to, I'm the same person. Well, my kids may get a grumpy mother every now and again. However, just as I'm responsible for them, I'm also responsible for my authors. And I know, because I'm an author, the challenges that authorship comes with. I know the highs and I know the lows.

I know how hard it is to build up a readership and to serve that readership. I know because I've been on this journey for 13 years. I wrote my first novel in 2010, and I have been learning ever since. The easy part is the writing.

So, I know. And I care. I could step back and just stay in my own words of authorship and not show up, but it is my duty to do otherwise.

It's my calling to show up. And that is why I'm a Heart Warrior and deserve a place in this book. Because, when you show up with love, you will do things that go above and beyond, that go wider and further than anyone else ever will. Because you care, because you want someone else to achieve. Because you want to show others. Part of the universal laws that I have studied over the years have taught me that when we learn, we're supposed to share our knowledge with others.

It's not for us to keep it a secret or lock it in a vault. Just like all the greedy guys who hid the gold in Aladdin's cave and kept all the golden nuggets to themselves. That's not sharing.

And yes, those guys may be rich in money, but are they rich in spirit? Are they happy? Joy and happiness are very important to me. If I ain't having fun, I ain't doing it. If it doesn't fulfil me, I ain't doing it.

But that does not mean that I have to be on a high all the time, not at all. I choose a higher vibration. I choose positivity. It takes work, it takes as much energy to be positive as it does to be negative, but I choose to be positive every day.

And tough challenges come and regardless of the perspective you approach them, they're still tough. So, embracing challenges and loving life, that's how we do it. And we bring other people along for the ride.

We stand alongside people. Inspired leadership is standing alongside people, not hovering over them. Standing alongside, not pushing out in front to get the medal. We stand alongside. That's what we do. We need to stand confidently in love so that they can stand confidently in love beside us. That's how it is. That's how it should always be.

So, no matter what it is that you want out of life, do it with love. No matter what it is that you think all those want from you, that's nothing to do with you. You just need to protect yourself, stay clear to your vision and bring those who are aligned with you along for the ride. It's your duty to keep your vibe high. It's your duty to keep your heart protected, your space protected, and remove toxic people from your life.

You are only responsible for yourself and how you react to things. This is what is important in life. Remember it.

Some takeaways from this chapter are:

1. To live as a Heart Warrior, one must prioritise self-care, mental health, and emotional intelligence. This includes developing a strong sense of self-awareness, practicing mindfulness, and cultivating a positive mindset.
2. Finding purpose is essential for living as a Heart Warrior. This involves identifying one's passions, values, and strengths, and aligning them with meaningful goals and actions that contribute to a greater good.
3. Embracing money is an important aspect of living as a Heart Warrior because it enables individuals to support themselves and others, fund their passions and goals and make positive contributions to society. When good people have money, they can do more good in the world.
4. To live as a Heart Warrior, it's important to take action in alignment with one's values and passions. This means learning to distinguish between opportunities that align with a "HELL yes" and those that are a "HELL no" and taking decisive action accordingly. This helps to avoid distractions and stay focused on what truly matters.

I valued connection and realised I had been playing it small. This led me to host a writer's retreat in a castle, which was profitable in its first year. However, we were still far from making a million dollars, and I didn't want to fake it until I made it. I wanted to show up authentically as a publisher, writer, mother and more.

My story shows the importance of setting intentions, being open to opportunities and staying true to yourself. It takes courage and a willingness to trust the journey, but the rewards can be great.

Writing my first heart-centred novel let me on a mission I knew would one day be bigger than me.

In conclusion, I want to share my story of how setting an intention and pairing it with a purpose, aligned with my values, led me to create something innovative and different. I am all about the journey and doing things differently. While it would be easier for me to just publish books and get them out into the world, that's not my focus. For me, publishing is just circumstantial.

People are drawn to me because I journey with them, but I have to be selective about who I journey with, because it can be draining. In 2010, I wrote my first novel, 'The Visitor,' which had my own personal story infused into it. It was a fictional novel that I wrote in 30 days, and everyone who read it said it was the answer their heart longed for. That's when I realised, I was a storyteller, and that my words could help others. I had a vision to build my own publishing press and give other authors a positive publishing experience.

I learned that a publishing experience is a journey, and it's not always positive. Challenges present themselves so that you can grow, and I was always open to that. I ended up with an entrepreneurial mindset and won awards along the way. All these things came from my intention.

I remember standing on my back patio, having set up my publishing press, starting to have authors come to me to get published. I felt in my zone of genius and purpose-driven, because not only was I helping make their dreams come true, but I was also on the journey alongside them. Authorship is undoubtedly a self-development journey, and sometimes it can get messy, but let's be honest, most worthwhile things do.

OVER THE EDGE IN FAITH

HELEN GLEN

I was born in an era when polio was an epidemic, it hit the world three times and unfortunately, as a small baby, I didn't escape this terrible virus.

Despite polio leaving me with a permanent facial droop, my mother always taught me to just get on with life. She was the one who gave me the courage and wisdom to know that I mattered as a person and that instead of making excuses, I just needed to do my best to succeed. I guess you could say that my darling mother was my rock.

Encouraged by both my parents, when I was 20 years old, I left India and came to live in Australia. I learned how to fit into my new country by adapting to the customs and lifestyle, playing and working hard.

Being an entrepreneur, my journey entailed a range of many interesting businesses, both in the city centres, as well as in remote Australia, when I lived in Port Hedland and Groote Eylandt, up in the Gulf of Carpenteria.

My passion was to volunteer in community affairs, and I always ensured I gave back to society as much as I could. On one occasion, when I owned a string of fashion boutiques, I held a fashion parade in honour of my son's seven-year-old friend, who had passed away from complications after heart surgery performed by a world-famous heart specialist. As a result of the funds raised, I was able to donate enough to purchase two heart monitors for the Sydney Children's Hospital.

Unfortunately, this little boy's heart had mirrored chambers and during surgery, the medical specialist discovered the child had no chance of survival. I learnt from his mother that there was a shortage of heart monitors at the time, and he would have greatly benefited from one, so it was the least I could have done.

The love, encouragement and inspiration from my parents had a profound effect on my life. My mother was my best friend and I always looked to her for advice, as I felt she understood me and I always felt safe in her presence.

When I was just ten years old and in boarding school at Bishop Cotton Girls High School, Bangalore, I was given the sad news that my mother had been diagnosed with breast cancer.

As the eldest of three children, I remember seeing mum's long scar after they removed her right breast with cancer. Although I didn't fully understand what this illness was, I remember seeing the wound on her chest being dressed by the home-visit nurse and nearly fainted.

Thinking about what she was going through, I would often cry myself to sleep and was tortured by the imagination of a ten-year-old child, wondering things such as, "How long will my mother live? Will I ever see her again?"

It was undoubtedly a sad and lonely period of my life and being in boarding school hardly helped the matter. Boarding school had endless rules and regulations, and no real warmth that only a mother can give her daughter, or the love you find shared in a family environment. Instead, I had to learn to survive, fend for myself and comply with the rules, which in turn, only saddened me further.

The knowledge of my mother having cancer weighed heavily on my heart. My younger brother, who was eight and my adorable little sister, only two, were told that mum may not live very long and so began the process of mourning the loss of someone who was still alive, as all hope seemed lost.

But we can be so wrong in giving ourselves so much unnecessary heartache sometimes, as I did back then by thinking about the 'What ifs', whereas in reality, my mother lived until I was thirty and delighted to hold my baby, her granddaughter, in her arms.

I've never regretted the day my entire family came to join me in Australia, grasping at the opportunities to also live a beautiful and successful life in such a wonderful country.

Encouraged by my parents, I left University in Bangalore to immigrate to Australia, determined to experience a new and promising life on this continent.

Fortunately, I was able to sponsor my family and they followed me out soon afterwards. We came as fully paying immigrants and as British citizens but were not allowed any assistance from the government to find our feet, so we went to work immediately, setting the bar high.

Together we created happy family times and mum had a very successful ten years in our new homeland, before she eventually lost her life to secondary cancer. (However, we were able to celebrate 22 years of her life in remission before she was taken away).

At the time of her death, my father requested there to be no flowers, and instead asked mourners to donate to the Cancer Council. To say the least, we were heartbroken saying our final goodbye to our wonderful mother, it was particularly difficult because she was our greatest champion, our cheerleader.

Even though I cried my heart out from this loss, in a way I felt a strange kind of relief for her, knowing that mum's suffering from a long history of cancer had come to an end and she was no longer in any pain or discomfort.

My father was a returned veteran who fought in World War II as a Lieutenant Colonel. He commanded troops in the Middle East and returned home at the end of WW II in 1945. Dad suffered from PTSD, but despite this, he never spoke about the war. Most men didn't in those days, and it was very unfortunate and sad that he suffered this dreadful mental illness in silence.

Unfortunately, we often experienced the aftermath of the war through my father's violent and aggressive behaviour.

My father was a proud and handsome man. His army life had groomed him well - he always dressed immaculately and was very polite and courteous to everyone he met. Despite this front, it was heart-breaking to know that when PTSD affected his mood, he went off the rails, but only behind closed doors.

Unfortunately, my mother lived her life as a 'battered woman', which was not only traumatic for her, but also for our family.

I would try and rescue mum from dad's violent episodes and show her as much support as possible, which sometimes resulted in me being hit or injured from my father's blows as well. I even remember going to school as a day girl, with black eyes and swollen lips.

It was truly horrible, and I always tried to protect my mother who was a wise and beautiful woman. Fortunately, bringing the family to live in Australia put less stress on dad in his new environment, one in which he worked hard and enjoyed the new lifestyle.

Another trait of his PTSD illness was that dad couldn't hold down a job for too long, he held some very responsible well-paying leadership positions, but he would crack under the strain - succumbing to PTSD once again.

I remember the last time I saw my dad was when he boarded his final flight from Sydney back to Perth. It seemed like only yesterday that dad looked so fit and handsome in his grey suit.

A year after mum's death, my father decided to end his life and committed suicide. He used his own gun to shoot himself. Sadly, I believe this was yet another effect of PTSD.

Coming to terms with my father's unexpected suicide was met with profound sadness by my entire family. My father didn't really know how much he was loved and will never know how much he is missed. Was it really necessary for him to cut short his life?

No.
To this day, he is still greatly missed by all of us.
And so, life goes on, there are good days and some not-so-good ones.

Having moved to Sydney to start a family after living in the 'Australian Outback', I decided to start a home-based furniture business, which took off like a rocket and progressed to a seven-figure revenue company. And that was even before the internet.

Unfortunately, the company endured hard times during the global recession, with the financial aftermath taking its toll on my business and family.

During this time, my now ex-husband went to live overseas as a single father, taking no responsibility for his actions and leaving behind his children, who didn't know where he was, or if he was dead or alive.

We had no details of his whereabouts but learned through mutual friends that he had gone to live in Russia.

By cutting himself off from us so suddenly, the shock caused my son to fret. He constantly worried about his father's safety, which led to his mental state deteriorating. When he started trialling drugs to help him forget his pain, they only made him more depressed and suicidal, which in turn, led to other problems.

It was not easy for me; I can tell you.
Mental illness is a silent and invisible illness.

My son was only in year eleven, but already he was in and out of hospital and school. My brother saw to it that my son continued to attend school, which was one of the finest in Australia, and all I could do was try to move forward and support him in every way possible.

My favourite cousin would often call around and keep an eye on us, he was the sweetest senior male member in the family and was well-respected. One of my fondest memories was him coming over with his son one evening and gifting me a basket of fresh peaches, straight from a farm he had visited earlier that day.

Strangely, on that same visit and completely out of the blue, he had said "Helen, if anything should happen to me, please take care of my sons."

A few months later, one hot summer's evening, he took his family, two boys and his wife, to the beach on the Northern Beaches of Sydney.

They had been having a great time, when suddenly, his youngest son got caught in a rip. My cousin was able to rescue him by swimming out and throwing him into the arms of a person swimming close by, but much to everyone's horror, my cousin was caught by the rip and taken out to sea.

It was late and the lifeguards had left for the day, Fortunately, however, some of them were at the pub across the road from the beach and one of them grabbed his rescue boat. Eight kilometres out to sea, he found my cousin and brought him back to shore, as his two young sons and wife looked on in horror and total disbelief.

Yes, my cousin saved his son's life, but sadly the lifeguards who worked frantically to resuscitate him, couldn't save him as he had swallowed too much salt water out in the vast ocean.

And so once again, we were mourning the death of yet another dear family member.

I assisted my cousin's wife and sons as much as I could. The boys had adored their father, he played cricket with them and was hands-on in his parenting, so it was difficult to see their small tear-stained faces mourning his loss.
Grief comes in all forms to all who love. Nevertheless, their father would be very proud of his sons today to know that they are now grown

men, contributing to society, and working in responsible jobs. The oldest son who works in telecommunications was able to share his extensive intelligence and knowledge of the industry through the discovery of a technological breakthrough that meant mobile signals could now be received in the midst of bush fires. The son saved by his father, is a strapping and successful lad, who although suffers from Asperger syndrome, is very intelligent and owes his life to his father's courageous effort.

Slowly, my life returned to normal, and my children and I finally felt settled and ready for the next chapter in our lives. I chose to live in a lovely leafy suburb of Sydney, in a resort-style complex, so we could play tennis, swim, and socialise. Fortunately, the country furniture store I had established had given us our livelihood and provided this somewhat luxe lifestyle. Little did we know however, that once again, our lives were to be turned upside down.

It was an autumn day in late April and my old Volvo wouldn't start, so I ended up hitching a lift to work with my daughter.

I tried all morning to call my son, as I wanted to let him know the mechanic would be calling around and to give him the keys to my car, but he wasn't answering his phone.

That afternoon I was mulling over my desk, rifling through paperwork, when my receptionist came and whispered in my ear, "Helen can you come with me please to the board room, there are two Police detectives here to see you."

My thoughts instantly went to my son, and I thought, "What has he done now?" The detectives asked me to sit down, saying they had some bad news, but I was not prepared for the terrible news they shared.

"Helen," they said, "Your son has been found dead, it is too early for us to give you more information at this stage". They had to repeat this news twice before what they were saying really sank in.

WHEN I WAS GIVEN THIS HEART-WRENCHING NEWS I WENT INTO TOTAL SHOCK, I PLEADED WITH GOD FOR IT NOT TO BE POSSIBLE.

I couldn't believe it.

"Please, God, don't let it be possible, oh please God, it's not true, it can't be true," I blurted out, sobbing, and reaching my arms towards the heavens.

My son was tragically killed only two months after my cousin's drowning, both their losses were unexpected and devastating for our whole extended family.

When my eldest daughter was informed of this tragic news over the phone, she was at work and fainted in the arms of her manager, the shock too much.

She came straight over to meet me, and we hugged each other, sobbing, and mourning together in overwhelming grief. The detectives, who were very supportive, didn't leave us and accompanied us home, as we still had to break the news to my youngest daughter.

That moment still pains me to this day, as my daughters and their brother were so close, they even shared mutual friends. Needless to say, my youngest daughter was devastated. Our world came crashing down and I wondered if life could get any worse. It felt as though my son took my broken heart to the grave with him.

As a mother, I missed him terribly, the pain was physically intense and I felt as though someone had put their hand through my chest, grabbed my heart and squeezed it, until it bled dry. It was a literal heart-ache. As Heart Warriors, we mothers, women and tribes, know how to love our children.

You cannot believe what it's like to lose a child, unless you experience this yourself, and I certainly do not wish it upon any mother, or parent, for that matter.

With tears rolling down my cheeks, I looked upwards towards the sky and asked 'The Divine' for mercy and blessings, to keep me strong until the day I would also see my beloved child again in the life thereafter.

I realised I could not focus on myself, nor dwell in grief, too much. I had to pull myself together to provide for my two beautiful daughters, who were still at school and in my sole care, so I returned to work two weeks after this tragedy.

I worked hard to support our diminishing family unit and to provide for the three of us. I did this while I also studied and added more complimentary holistic modalities to my portfolio that would increase my knowledge to help others in the future.

I never thought I would recover from the depths of pain, the depths of despair and the depths of grief, but it's true that we can heal ourselves compassionately, while recognising that healing takes time and that everyone is unique in how they deal with loss and sadness.

I realised how fortunate I was to have raised a boy, to have seen him grow into a loveable teenager, with a sense of humour that we and his friends loved.

How different he was from his sisters and his steadfast love of nature always impressed me. One day as a kindergarten student, he brought home a box of caterpillars from school, to look after over the weekend, diligently feeding them mulberry leaves from a tree nearby. It's something I'll never forget, and I know if he was here today, he'd be working with animals.

It is true that I understand what it is like to live on the edge of a 'new normal' life, yet now I also feel inspired to live it meaningfully.

After running my own successful multi-million-dollar enterprise, in partnership with my ex-husband, the business partnership ended with a failing marriage and culminated in a nasty divorce.

I was too afraid to allow the trauma of what I went through with financial ruin to rule my life, so I continued to study and worked in marketing for Corporate Australia.

Along the way, I learnt quite a few things about breaking patterns of co-dependency, overcoming sleepless nights and low self-esteem, all of which were lessons that in turn, helped soothe my bleeding heart.

Journaling was a way of whispering my thoughts and releasing deep pain of grief I felt during dark times, and I learnt to accept life in my new normal, by allowing grief to live alongside me.

Journaling also allowed me to speak to my son through my heart, it helped me get to sleep on those restless nights and it allowed me to pour out all the heartfelt stories of grief I felt.

When I wrote a letter to my son, it helped soothe my breaking heart night after night, and it was only after writing down how I felt, that I was able to finally find relief.

I found journaling so beneficial that I decided to create a The 5 star rated 'Women's Think And Grow Journal' to keep you accountable, motivated and inspired, for bigger, bolder, higher goals.

People often ask me, 'What was a turning point in life for you Helen?" and I say it was that I found my soulmate by allowing love to come into my life again, because I eventually remarried and my husband and I live happily in Sydney, Australia.

So how did our romance begin?

I was a sole parent but had strong relationships with my friends. One day we decided to hire a yacht with skipper and sail around Pittwater. The clear blue skies completed a beautiful summer's day in Newport, while the yacht gently swayed on the shimmering water.

It was here, I looked up and saw standing on the bow of the yacht, a gentleman I had never seen before. As our eyes fleetingly met, little did

I know I had just met the man of my dreams, who would go on to steal my heart and make me his bride.

And to this day, my husband and I happily reside in a quiet bay side suburb of Sydney.

I am proud and grateful that both my daughters have grown up to be independent, beautiful, strong women living their lives successfully.

We are in close contact with each other, and when we come together to celebrate occasions, often end up giggling about the things their brother did and spoke. To us, my sons' memory will never die, he made us laugh and as the girls say, "He was our clown".

Life has its ups and downs, and more recently there have been many global changes, with drastic consequences for many. As we all know when COVID-19 hit the world by storm, we experienced things that we never imagined would ever take place.

Once again, I too felt the tug of the universe convincing me to give up my 9-5 marketing job and return to my studies. This time around, I listened and have since become an accredited International Results Coach, Grief Counsellor and Speaker.

There is HOPE for those who want HELP.

Mindfulness and meditation are a holistic approach to healing, and are important healing tools that when used effectively, can lift the mood of your soul to another level. Though we can never forget our loved ones whom we grieve for, we can learn to live happily with all the precious memories they gave us.

I was quite happy to adopt a way of living in my 'new normal' by practising rituals that helped me cope. Before meeting my second husband, I took time off, packed up and moved to the Gold Coast, along with my youngest daughter, for a year. This was where I could run on the beach, breathe in the fresh air, and live a more relaxed lifestyle than I did in Sydney. This was also a refreshing respite from the stress of awaiting the outcome of the court matter, which took two years to finish.

I need not have attended any of these court cases, as the government represented me, demanding justice on my behalf and I was also given support from people in the Homicide Victims group meetings and other organisations, but I'm getting ahead of myself here and suppose I better fill in the blanks, as raw as they are to talk about.

The fateful night my son died, he happened to be in the wrong place, at the wrong time. Although the perpetrator received life imprisonment, he was allowed out after four years in jail, because he showed such remorse about killing a man he didn't even know. To be honest, it really didn't matter, nor did I really care, what degree of justice the perpetrator was served, because my heart was full of sorrow for my son. I would never see him again and no one could ever return him to me.

I was there for my son in life, and I was there for him in death.
Death is final.
Life can be a bitch.
Deep grief takes its toll.
I did everything to help myself to heal my broken heart.
But it continues to be painful.

I created a place of healing, a sacred 'healing altar' at home, where I could find solace, meditate, pray and feel connected in spirit to my child. My little altar was my sacred place, it was just a special table, with a beautiful tablecloth, where I placed my favourite photograph of my son.

I'd buy fresh flowers, light a candle, and spend time reflecting on what my son really and truly meant to me, how much I missed him and how difficult it was, and still is, to live without him. And then I'd move on for the day, as I knew there were others who needed me.

Shedding a few tears and talking to my boy in my journal, also made me feel better, and I did this for as long as it took to heal after a loss.

I BELIEVE I AM NOW LIVING OVER THE EDGE IN FAITH.

Replacing sad thoughts with something that makes you laugh changes your mood in an instant, and it is an incredible feeling.
Try it, it really works.

A happier future awaits you, but you must name it and claim it, for it to happen. To experience the metamorphosis of coming through overwhelming grief, to becoming passionate about living life with confidence and clarity, as well as becoming a successful female business entrepreneur, spells FREEDOM.

Please, be the next woman to get the results you desire. To find what makes you happy. To find your freedom. BECAUSE YOU ARE SO WORTHY.

I AM LIFE ITSELF

PEIMING SUN

Self-discovery through adversities!

I was NOT a happy person growing up. When I was 14, I still vividly remember one of my middle school friends shouting at me for complaining that I did not have enough of EVERYTHING. My parents also often commented that I was a demanding child, who was unable to feel satisfied from a very young age.

Little did I know that these were actually key elements for me to embody my authentic self and align my life purpose, as a holistic lifestyle mentor.

I guide people over 40, to live with sustainable life energy, authenticity, clarity, and happiness. Based on my life experience, I have integrated phototherapy technology, ancient traditions, and habit building, for midlife transformation.

At 55 years old, I have finally realised that I am, like any other human and anything else that exists, ENOUGH and PERFECT for what I set to accomplish and flourish on earth. Thus, I am LIFE itself.

There are five major phases that I have experienced to reach my realisation that I am LIFE itself. I would like to share my HEAD-to-HEART journey with you as a Heart Warrior and invite you to honour and embody your inherent inner wisdom, and live with sustainable life energy, clarity and happiness.

The 1st phase: Why me?

As humans, we have expectations, anticipations, dreams, hope, desire, goals and aspirations. My aspiration to come to the USA in 1991 from Taiwan, was also to become a great molecular biologist, who could bring DNA technology to solve people's long-term health issues, such as cancer, ageing and memory loss.

All things were going well when my journey first started. I successfully obtained my Master of Science degree in 1993, married a man whom I deeply adored in 1994, became a mother in 1995 and landed a well-compensated corporate job as a molecular biologist in a large pharmaceutical company in 1998. Everything was flowing smoothly and effortlessly.

Then, directed by a mysterious force, I had to give up my American dream through a series of major unfortunate events. I became a single mother with two young sons in 2000, after discovering my ex-partner was actually married to another woman in a different country. Then, in 2004, my second son was diagnosed with a genetic terminal disease, Duchenne Muscular Dystrophy (DMD). As a result, in 2008 I decided to quit my demanding corporate job to maintain my overall well-being and sanity as a single mother, without any assistance.

I was angry, sad, confused, stressed, isolated and depressed. I wasted lots of time asking, "Why me?" questions that I could not answer. My mind, dominated by the left side of my logical brain, was trying to make sense about what happened and wanted to solve all these problems, despite being a wounded and stressed lone warrior.

The 2nd phase - Fix and save me!

These unfortunate events confirmed my doubts about life, namely that I was inadequate, unlovable and could not live a happy life. Therefore, I decided to improve myself and prove that I can become a better version of ME.

I started a 20-year self-development journey to improve myself, through attending workshops, reading books, joining support groups and going to spiritual gatherings, offered by various religious groups. In addition, I also started a new relationship in 2005, hoping I could be taken care of and no longer need to feel lonely and unloved.

These steps might sound very logical to you. Perhaps you have done something similar, that is, seeking solutions and other people to fix and save yourself.

However, I found all these actions of trying to improve myself merely turning into a goose chase, and I established co-dependency on my happiness with people and events around me. As a result, I was unable to truly accept and love myself.

Per my understanding, after self-realisation, our ego or rooted fear is designed to protect us from danger and instead, seeks external solutions to solve problems. But, if we let our fear fully control our life, we will become someone who is constantly chasing the next tool, knowledge, practice, in the hope we can be fixed and saved.

The worst part of allowing fear to rule our life is that we also create the habit of comparing ourselves to others. Thus, in turn, we build a mental jail that traps us in this vicious cycle of self-criticism daily.

The 3rd phase: Stupid me!

Did I tell you that I have a Master of Science degree in Molecular Biology? Who cares, you might think. And yes, exactly, who cares?

True wisdom is completely different to knowledge we have learned and experienced. As a highly educated intellect, I have noticed that I did not necessarily have the right skills to deal with unexpected life events with intelligence. On the contrary, I used too much logic and an analytical mind to respond to situations prematurely, which in turn, ensnared me even deeper into the mental jail that I had built.

'Gene Keys', by Richard Rudd, an author who has been inspired by the ancient 'I-Ching or Book of Changes', has listed human's 64 archetypes, within the spectrum of consciousness: The Shadow, Gift and Siddhi, which represents our challenges, our creativity and our essence. Richard has also created the 'Golden Path' to represent our journey on Earth, that we are here to embrace or accept our shadows and express our gifts via our life's work, so ultimately, we can embody our rooted essence.

The 'Golden Path' is consistent with 11 spheres, three sequences and 12 inter-paths. For more information, check out Genekeys.com. As a Gene Keys Guide, I welcome you to connect with me for a short tour and introduction, so that you can start to explore and contemplate your unique Golden Path.

The shadow frequency of my culture Gene Key 62 is intellect. In ancient I-Ching, which has been around for more than 8000 years, this key is also a reminder to respect others, know our position as a human, whilst between heaven and earth, and not overact in any situation.

Looking back, I have invested more than $100K, spent more than twenty years of living with self-doubt and self-judgement, ignored my innate wisdom and essence, and lived my life based on my logical mind that is fed by my own illusions created from my fear.

I have actually turned into a self-obsessed being, who has false beliefs and repeats actions that don't benefit anyone. Can you relate?

There are two quotes from Albert Einstein that shifted my perspective at this phase:

"Insanity is doing the same thing over and over again and expecting different results."

"Any problem cannot be solved with the same level of consciousness that created it."

With the shifted awareness happening for me in early 2020, I finally started my quest of discovering ME.

The 4th phase - Who is me?

Do you really know who you are? I do not know who I am, but I am pretty sure I know who I am NOT.

Dr. Svante Paabo, the Nobel Prize winner of Physiology or Medicine in 2022, has shared that we are distinctly different from these extinct Hominins that have been discovered. Through the 13-year human genome project (1990-2003), we also became aware that we are not that 'advanced', compared to lower life forms at the genetic level.

As I could not find the answers by seeking external solutions, I chose to go inwards in early 2020, after experiencing spiritual awakening.

I have discovered that I am NOT the identity or belief system that I had held so closely, based on my appearance, age, sex, skills, job titles or degrees. I have been through so many roles and functions throughout my 55 years on earth and ditched some of my limiting beliefs. Yet, NONE of them can objectively and truly define ME.

I follow the Jamaican spiritual teacher, Mooji, for his simple and enlightened teaching about spirituality.

I particularly enjoy the examples he has shared many times, to prove the concept that our ego, or conditioned self, is a separate entity from our true self. He has asked people, "Although you are the sharpest knife and you can cut ANYTHING in the world, however, can you cut yourself?" This is just simple logic. If I can observe my thoughts or words, I must be a separate entity from the one who is thinking and saying. Thus, I am NOT my thoughts or words.

I also realise that I am NOT my emotions. Scientists have reported that people can be triggered to feel happy, excited, lonely, sad, angry, worried, or afraid, via electrical currents or certain chemicals in the laboratory setting. We can also have certain emotions in response to environmental triggers, or conditioned beliefs, based on our experience or habits.

Emotions are waves and I can strategically redirect these waves using pauses. As a Tiny Habits certified coach trained directly by Dr. BJ Fogg, a world-renowned behavioural scientist at Stanford University, I completely agree with his observation based on the extensive amount of collected data: Habit design is emotion design.

Thus, we are the co-creator of our emotions and habits, but we are NOT our emotions. The Tiny Habits method is a perfect tool to create strategic pauses in our daily routine, so that we can shift our emotions, live in the moment and become self-empowered, via its A-B-C formula: Anchor Moment, Behavior and Celebration.

Last but not least, I have become fully aware that I am NOT even my physical body. Gee, this concept was not easy for me to grasp at first. I need to credit the modern scientific breakthroughs and ancient traditions that have helped me tremendously to reach this realisation.

The Nobel Prize of Physics in 2022 was granted to three physicists, Alain Aspect, John Clauser, Anton Zeilinger, who have dedicated their lives to conducting numerous experiments over decades, to explain quantum entanglement, a phenomenon in which entangled systems exhibit correlations that cannot be explained by classical physics.

When applying this phenomenon at a cellular level, each cell that has been created from the same fertilised egg, is a fractal reality entanglement with the entire body. Yet, it is not our body. Our body contains trillions and trillions of cells and every seven years, it renews every single cell, based on an inner self-regulated system. Our ancestors from various cultures had documented similar findings for thousands of years, and have used ways to disentangle certain trapped energy, to cure diseases and save lives.

We are energetic and limitless beings. Our bodies, which are built with 99.9% energy, formed by layers of sound waves or energy fields, emit certain frequencies to connect with others and the Universe. When our physical body is not in sync with the vibrations of nature, then we will experience pain, stress, or pressure. All of which act as a reminder for us to become more coherent or synchronised with the Source.

Therefore, I really do not know who I am, yet I know from the bottom of my heart that I am not my identity and belief system. I am everything, as everything is energy, and nothing can actually be used to define ME.

The 5th phase - I am life itself!

In late 2021, I was introduced to an amazing system that incorporates quantum science, ancient wisdom, physiology, astrology, and genetics. It is called the Human Design System. The founder and messenger Ra Uru Hu, now deceased, had an incredible downloading experience in 1987, then created this integrated system in just eight days.

As a molecular biologist, I have a particular interest in one of the aspects of the Human Design System, 'Gene Keys'. As I mentioned before, 'Gene Keys' is a book written by Richard Rudd. It is also a holistic synthesis system that integrates Ancient I-Ching 64 archetypes into 64 Gene Keys, Genetics, Quantum Physics, Biology, Chemistry, Poetry, and Astrology. Basically, it is all about LIFE and gentle ways to balance our left-logic and right-creative brain for synchronicity and coherence with the Universe, the Source.

My purpose key is Key 57, with line 3. Based on my daily contemplation, I come here to share messages like a gentle wind and guide others through the four elements of The Gene Keys Approach: Gentleness, Patience, Contemplation, and Inquiry. Yet, I need to experience many trials and errors, so I too can become wiser and in turn, share these stories to guide others.

Applying the 'Gene Keys' approach, I have gradually embodied some of my rooted essence, realised my natural gifts, self-healed, ditched the unhealthy relationship that lasted for 17 years in 2022 and accepted my purpose as a Holistic Lifestyle Mentor.

All the adversities I encountered were my unseen grace that I needed to embrace and experience. The ME is just a fractal conditioned self, or 64 shadows with lower frequency, that resonates with the collective human suffering experience. Therefore, I am NOT ME either.

As energetic beings, we can activate and regenerate our natural and powerful capacities that have been suppressed or taken away by our unhealthy modern lifestyle and false beliefs.

We do not need to be fixed, as we have rooted essence and superpowers, yet we need to stay open, upgrade our perspectives, take proper actions to build good habits, trust in ourselves and LIFE so that we can holistically become in sync with the Universe.

It is my purpose, after self-realisation, to share my wisdom and approach with people over 40, who currently live with loaded stress and false beliefs, so that they can start to live with authenticity, sustainable life energy, clarity, and happiness.

My purpose is actually still resonating with my original aspiration in 1991, which was to become a scientist that bridges technology and human suffering. However, it has shifted from the molecular to quantum level, accordingly in the 21st century.

I have integrated 'Gene Keys' teaching that can raise self-awareness at the quantum level, as well as the Tiny Habits Method to implement good habits and phototherapy technology to maintain our DNA and stem cell health, regenerating sustainable energy needed for individual and planetary transmission.

I am hosting free and paid events, masterclasses, retreats and other virtual and local programs. I believe transformation happens in a supportive community and I am confident that I can effectively guide others to shift perspectives and embrace LIFE with ease.

You are welcome to join us, as you are an important piece of the puzzle for us to reach global PEACE collectively.

HIT ME AGAIN, I CAN TAKE IT

SHARON LYNNE

So, what happens when a thriving stage and media career blooms for thirty-six years and then just wilts…no, more like *'hits a wall at full force?'*

That's exactly what happened to me.

Always led by a passion for music and entertainment, I soared to the top of my musical theatre career and bathed in the glory of applause and bright lights, playing lead roles in National Opera houses. But the political climate in my home country of South Africa, abruptly forced me to turn a corner. Not a bend, a sharp corner.

As passionate and in love as I was with the world of entertainment, I loved my two sons more. I knew that it was more important for them to experience a life surrounded by peace and a strong sense of security, in contrast to living behind ten-metre-high walls and never being able to safely ride their bikes around the neighbourhood streets. In 1996, South Africa was volatile. Millions of deprived people were living with years of pent-up anger and thousands of privileged-others with new-founded fear.

It was a massive decision I had to make, as painful as it was. I knew I had to walk away from a flourishing career at thirty-six years old.

Time after time, I had been chosen to play the lead in many well-known musicals, performing sought after roles like Eva Peron in Evita, Nancy in Oliver and Nellie Forbush in South Pacific, to name a few. Now, I had to focus on my priorities and not my passion. It was crunch time.

It all came to a head on my way back from work one night, when I found my car suddenly surrounded by a group of six angry men, whilst stationary at a traffic light. My doors were locked for obvious reasons. The group rocked my car ferociously and I knew then I had only two options. To stay and be robbed of my car or even worse, possibly killed and then robbed, or put my foot on the pedal and get out of there. I did not hesitate. I chose the latter and went straight through a red traffic light.

I arrived home unharmed and informed my husband at the time that we were no longer safe in this country and had to leave immediately. Before I knew it, we had immigrated to Australia, with very little.

It was not easy on arrival. This time I was not suffering from stage fright, but culture shock, and it took every ounce of my strength to pass the endurance test. I dug deep and it's times like this that you soon find out how to dodge the bullets. To put it simply, although it was anything but simple, my marriage was short-lived and I was now in this quagmire alone, with two small mouths to feed.

Suffering from newly developed panic attacks, I set about trying to find an income. Not just by 'getting a job' though, I have never worked for someone else, and all things considered, was not about to start. Yet, I still knew I needed to follow my gut. I had a burning passion to succeed once again, on different shores and facing a mountain of adversity I had not yet contemplated.

But my feet no longer fitted those glittery shoes. With no top billing in Australia, agents turned me away. Television channels used me as bait for one of their documentaries about auditioning for a lead role, edited in a profoundly biased way, which left me professionally scarred.

It was a rude awakening.
I had to learn to swim in much deeper waters.
So, to survive, I decided to do what most performers do: Teach.

Most people don't know that I had already been teaching since the age of seventeen. After acquiring my qualifications, as both a dance and drama teacher, I realised now was the perfect opportunity to be successful again as a teacher, but this time as a teacher of my long-practised 'other' passion: Presenting.

In South Africa, because of my stage profile, I was invited to present a few TV programs including music, entertainment, and children's educational shows, so I had learned how to become a presenter whilst 'on the job'.

It was something I found quite natural and once again, started making a name for myself in the broadcasting industry. During this period, I had also been training talent in South Africa to become presenters, so I thought, why not just continue doing the same in Australia?

Surely it was a no-brainer. Or was it? After all, I had been presenting for a few years prior to leaving South Africa. I had discovered how to truly connect to an audience and the positive feedback I received, convinced me that I had formulated unique techniques, hence it didn't take long to realise I could teach these specialised techniques that no-one else in Australia was teaching. So, I jumped right into the deep end.

With an emphasis on a story-telling delivery, a conversational style of communications and an intimate viewer-connection, which wasn't journalism, I opened up TV Pro Global (initially called Sharon Lynne Televisions Promotions) in South Africa. This unique point of difference was how I established myself as a media trainer with the focus on presentation delivery through the lens of a camera.

My passion for developing raw talent was what drove me and continues to drive me today. I was innately born with the gift of recognising a person's strengths. I thrive on showing students how to exhibit their natural talent, using techniques that enhance their true connection and likability factor. This is one of the reasons I have always enjoyed teaching, as it presents an opportunity for me to bring out other people's strengths, using my own.

But it was not long-lasting joy, because six months into establishing my training studio in a large room of a rented home, I heard a banging on my front door and was confronted by television cameras and a tight-lipped journalist with an 'Out-to-get-you attitude'.

I was accused of being unqualified and making money off unsuspecting candidates. I was furious. In fact, my 'anger Richter scale' was off the charts. I had not endured the challenging pain of emigration, culture shock and the resurrection of my life for myself and my two kids, to be annihilated by this seemingly sanctimonious presenter, who had obviously not done her research.

Drawing on my acting experience, I smiled and invited the journalist and her team to interview me, knowing full well I was not going to allow her to break me the way that the channel had tried to, when they interviewed me in their documentary called "Audition". This was filmed just after my arrival into Australia. I turned the interview right around, as one does if you know how to handle being interviewed by the media and proceeded to interview the journalist on her ability to retain credibility and authenticity within her stories. I vividly remember politely adding, "Because you have not done your research on my background. So, when you do, I would encourage you to seek legal advice before you air your distorted story of blame.

This segment was never aired, and I often wonder what took place after they left. One thing's for sure though, whoever that journalist was, she left me alone to continue my (now very successful) career as a trainer. So, "Hit me again, I can take it"

Fortunately, through tenacity and hard work, I was able to give my children a wonderful, safe, secure, and loving upbringing, whilst operating a business I had initiated out of passion, rather than desperation.

If you talk to people who want to be in the limelight, either as a performer or presenter, you will discover that there are many who suffer from performance anxiety, as I had suffered throughout my career. But because I mastered controlling my stage fright, I also help students rise above their fear, so that their strengths as a presenter can overshadow their nerves. I have now formulated strategic techniques which is an integral part of my training.

If you've ever experienced that 'breakthrough' moment as a trainer, you will know it's that 'Aha' moment you wait for. I am sure you can relate to what I'm now describing. There is no turning back after this moment. To witness that metamorphosis has become my go-to-drug. It is my tonic. My inspiration. It is why I do what I do.

If I don't operate with purpose and passion, then I am wasting precious time. Life is way too short to indulge in mediocrity. So, what do I mean? For me, it's when you just do things to …well…just exist. Of course, routine is important to keep on track, as is self-discipline and organisation.

But without the purpose behind the passion, the strategy behind the idea, the fuller vision behind your goal, you are probably compromising or possibly procrastinating. So, my suggestion is return to the drawing board and explore all your options. Don't be afraid to take calculated risks. Failure is part of succeeding. I know you've heard that before.

But have you *actually* tried it?

Don't let me lose track of the story, as I want to talk about other important things I have invited into my life. After another fifteen years of juggling kids, business and money, I soon realised I was lacking a work-life balance for myself. What else did I need? More motivation? More excitement? I wasn't sure, but one thing I was certain of was that I had knocked myself out, trying to stay on top of my game as a trainer and casting agent.

I spent as much quality time as possible with my children in between work, being there for their soccer games, their Taekwondo lessons and making them home baked dinners each night.

But being a career mother never feels like you're doing enough. There is always a lingering measure of guilt. One thing I was proud of though, was that I had raised my two ADHD boys in a secure and comfortable environment, albeit far away from their mother country, but for all the right reasons. They were well-balanced happy children.

Nevertheless, I continued to feel this inner nagging and I knew it was time for either another career change, or more work-life balance. Procrastination and compromise had already started rearing their ugly heads. But what did work-life balance look like when I only knew how to work long hours? I had become obsessive with work and it was starting to consume not only my time, but also my soul. I did not know what a break looked like. Both my children were growing up fast, finding their niches and breaking away to do their own thing. So, it was time to realise my passion that was going to take me through the next phase of my life.

One night I sat down with a bottle of 'Taylors' Shiraz, a book and a pen (because I'm old fashioned) and started writing down a list of my passions. It went something like this:

Travelling – Not enough time for regular travel, but something that I could come back to.
Musical theatre – Been there, done that.
Musical instrument – It didn't do much for me anymore.
Reading – Loved it, but it was static stimulation.

There were other things on the list that didn't excite me, until I wrote it down: ANIMALS.
It hit me like a freight train, and I knew then and there that I wanted to work with animals.

But I also knew that was not going to keep the roof over our heads, especially as I had no zoological qualifications. I had another few sips of wine and then the penny dropped.

Volunteering! I would pick my favourite animal and find a sanctuary to volunteer at once a year. That way I could still continue with TV Pro Global.

After another long list, this time of animals, I decided on orangutans and for seven years, I have been volunteering at two incredible orangutan sanctuaries in Borneo. Does it give me work-life balance? You bet it does. Working with orangutans not only fulfilled a much-needed gap in my life, but also ticked off a bucket list dream.

There was much more to this that I had not anticipated. I met likeminded people from all over the world, who had the same passion for orangutans and animal protection, and I learned so much more about critically endangered species, orangutans being amongst that list. I became frighteningly aware of illegal deforestation and how it impacts all of our lives, let alone the diminishing animal kingdom. As I became more and more involved with their rescue, rehabilitation, and release, I became increasingly passionate and mesmerised by these incredible animals.

I was eventually invited to go on an actual release, which meant I had to travel for twenty-five hours in a convoy of trucks, carrying five rehabilitated orangutans who were finally going to experience their freedom in their true forest home. They had been rehabilitating at the sanctuary for the past six to seven years and were finally ready to return to nature.

Most of the orangutans at the sanctuary were tiny babies, lying next to the bloodied body of their mother, and had been collected from the floor of a burned-out forest, which had been illegally cleared for palm oil plantations. These poor defenceless baby orangutans were more often than not, illegally trafficked by poachers, as many thousands still are. This time though, the Borneo Orangutan Survival Foundation in Kalimantan, Borneo, got to them first.

Working with these beautiful creatures had finally ignited another of my passions I didn't know existed. Passion that would inject enough motivation in me to cope with the rest of my world back home.

Nowadays, life is easier. My youngest son has a great career and is now happily married and planning to buy his first home this year. I'm already expecting there'll be a few grandchildren to come. My eldest son is about to be engaged and is also on his way to launching a career in his chosen profession. I feel content. In my heart and mind, I have done the best I can, and I have finally reached a stage in my life where I no longer carry any guilt.

I believe I have earned the right to feel accomplished, both as a mother and as a career professional. I did not allow negative circumstances, false accusations, or intermittent adversity to tarnish my vision, disrupt my sense of survival or, most importantly, kill my passion. This is not a full stop. I will never stop looking to colour-in my life's canvas, with opportunity fuelled by passion. So, once again, I have embarked on another career subsidiary and at the mature age of sixty-eight, I am studying to become a travel journalist.

Go on life, hit me again, I can take it.

MY PHILOSOPHY OF LIFE

PATRICIA JO GROVER

First, I want to say hello to you my fellow Heart Warrior, and secondly, know that you are not alone. If you are reading this book, it is because you were destined to. Maybe because you need to be exposed to the content, to gain a realisation of some sort to help you need, or perhaps you need to gain clarity and feel empowered, to take the necessary steps, in a positive direction, to move forward into the next chapter of your life.

We are who we are today and have become what we have become, because of what we have experienced previously in our lives. Saying this, I ask you to close your eyes for a few brief seconds and allow yourself to have a quick flashback of what some of these things were for you.

This will help you to maybe understand a little about my 'Philosophy of Life' being like a jigsaw puzzle. Having all those pieces being part of not only making up who we are today, but also the results of having experienced them and how it has given us the wisdom, knowledge and courage to help us to continue to put the pieces, that still are laying out on the table in front of us, together.

None of us know for sure what our future holds for us, and what our 'Jigsaw Puzzle' is going to look like when it is completed. More often than not, it ends up being a collage of our life's experiences of the good, the bad, the ugly, and the beautifully wonderful.

You can read more in depth about my 'Philosophy of Life' in my writings, 'Living Outside the Box', 'Ride or Die', and 'Being the Love of Your Own Life'.

I just want to take a moment to share how I developed this philosophy and how it pertains to being a "Heart Warrior".

Some of you reading this may have realised that, hey I've seen this lady before somewhere, or have heard of her, others will be discovering who I am and what I do, for the very first time. Now, I want to go back to what I said in the very beginning and discuss the meaning of being a 'Heart Warrior' as understood by me.

I believe that deep inside each of our souls, we have a yearning to love and to be loved, to share and to be accepted. But I have also realised that life happens to every single one of us, whether we are ready for it or not.

By saying this bold statement, it is a way of explaining that things happen as and when they should, we cross paths with some people, situations, or circumstances that have changed the course of our lives. This can be either good or bad, depending on your perspective.

My journey through life began with many negative things and my childhood experiences affected me well into adulthood. I never knew what a healthy, happy home life was supposed to be like, let alone what a healthy relationship was supposed to look like.

Because of the lack of knowing these things, yet my heart and soul desiring them, I set out to discover through a string of relationships with other people, over many years. Unfortunately, I only found myself in unhealthy situations.

I found that I was looking for that special something in another person that would make me feel whole. So there ended up being a lot of trial and error. That ended in three failed marriages, a child, a couple of committed relationships, and one engagement that ended rather abruptly. This all happened because my heart and soul were still searching and fighting to find what I truly wanted, needed, and desired in my life.

It wasn't until after my third divorce that I said to myself enough is enough. Yet, why I couldn't find love and happiness continued to perplex me. I'm a smart, intelligent, hardworking, decent, honest and attractive woman, but there was obviously something wrong with me as I hadn't been able to find what I'd been looking for from any of these relationships. What pieces of this puzzle was I just not seeing?

This is the point that my 'Philosophy of Life' was beginning to take shape.

Because at that point, I had looked back at everything from my past and chosen to learn from it. I didn't want to continue to live in the insanity of doing the same things over and over and expecting different results.

Every single man that I had tried to have a relationship with were all totally different, it wasn't like I kept going after the same type.

So, I had to decide to be vulnerable enough with myself to be completely honest, no matter how painful that was going to be. To break down all the pieces of my puzzle that had made my life what it had been to that point.

This is where my notes came from that I used when I decided to start writing my first book. It was these notes that aided me in the development of the first prototypes of the products and services that I have made available on my platform to aid others.

You see back then, as a single mother in her late 20's, there really weren't many, if any, women out there writing self-help books or doing motivational speaking. So, I read and listened to what I could that was being shared by the men out there, in that genre at that time and took away as much as I could, using it in a way that only benefitted my life. This is how my journey of learning to understand the 'Know, Like, Trust' method, and ultimately loving myself, began. Along the way, I found that I had to make tweaks and changes to how I was talking to myself, and to the things that I was doing to support my growth.

Again, these things I refer to as the products and services that I now call part of my proprietary, 'Conquering Skills Education'.

Once I started applying these life changes, I started to notice a shift towards the positive, because I had begun to take these steps to re-take, re-shape and re-make my life. I knew in my heart that I was on the right track.

Eventually, I began having incremental wins that encouraged and empowered me to continue to grow, both personally and professionally.

Having those wins also bolstered my confidence, allowing me to become more curious about what opportunities may be ahead of me. It was then that I had my 'Ah-ha' moment. If I had been able to have such wonderful results by following a system that I had created for myself, why wouldn't this benefit others? Surely, I couldn't be THAT different from everyone else. I know that there are many people out there that have experienced things much worse than me, and others who haven't experienced enough. So, this was why I thought about writing a book to share my 'Philosophy of Life' and the 'System' that I had been creating.

Now, nine years later, I am still experiencing personal and professional growth, and as a result, I decided to start dating again. I joined Match.com and put my wish list out there. My profile didn't say, "I like to take moonlight strolls on the beach barefoot". No, it said, "My man must be…, have…, do…, not do…, want…., and like…".

Because at this point, I had gotten to 'Know, Like, Trust', and love myself enough that I knew exactly what I wanted, needed, and desired in my partner in life.

I even put in the profile that if this isn't you, don't bother to respond!

Yes, you can laugh out loud with me, or even at me, for having the audacity to feel like I I had the right to put that kind of profile out there, but I knew at that point that I was worthy of having that special someone. That all the work I had done on and for myself had paid off and I finally deserved to have those desirable pieces of the puzzle fit with that special person.

Now, I want to share with you all that posting that profile wasn't the 'magic wand moment' that made my prince appear.

There were still many toads that leapt into my life, and a few got kissed, until one day a man answered saying, "I'm pretty sure it's me that you are looking for".

We started having conversations through Match, then via text and phone calls, prior to me agreeing that I'd like to meet him in person.

He asked me out on our first date on Valentine's Day, but I couldn't make myself go, because to me, you only spent time out celebrating that day with your someone special.

He, I found out after the fact, was hurt that I had not wanted to show up that night and I ended up hearing about it jokingly for years.

You see, we did end up going on our first date 10 days later. There were so many things that led to that date that it was almost synchronicity, even things that happened during the date seemed serendipitous. My dear friends, a husband and wife, knew all that I had been through and said that they needed to meet and approve of this guy before I went on another date with him.

So, our second date was with them, assessing whether or not he was up to their standards, so to speak. AS they were leaving, they both gave me their approval.

It was on our third date that he asked me to marry him.

Not as an actual proposal with a ring, but that was when we were no longer just ourselves. At this point we were both committed to living the rest of our lives 'Happily Ever After' together. But this isn't where the story book ends, my fellow "Heart Warriors. "Because we all know that 'Life happens to every single one of us whether we are ready for it or not'.

We created a wonderful life together and were reaping all the benefits, until I had a bad motorcycle accident and am lucky to be here now and be writing this. There is more about this that I share in some of my other writings.

After my recovery, we decided that life was too short and that we should do something that we both had on our bucket list. And life continued to bring many ups and downs and as we experienced it all, we held onto one another for dear life, enjoying every single minute of it.

In November of 2017, my partner was diagnosed with Mantle Cell Lymphoma and was given between two to five years to live. Regardless of the diagnosis, we chose not to let this stop us from enjoying every minute of the time we still had together. In fact, the week he was diagnosed was the week I started writing my first book.

Sadly, my love was taken from me by the 'Powassan Virus' on March 23, 2022.

Which brings me to accept the fact that I have undoubtedly earned the title of "Heart Warrior" and know that I am more than equipped to help others who are on a similar path in life.

I continue to live my life, 'Purposefully, Joyfully, and Gratefully', and believe I am serving the world and showing everyone how they can reach their own full potential while they do the same.

PANACHE DESPITE CIRCUMSTANCES

KELLY MARKEY

In many ways, women have reinforced, fashioned, developed, revolutionised, and crafted the world as it contours our daily landscape. Womenfolk are conscientious for some of our world's paramount successes and continue to subsidise and structure the way that our world works. Performing these undertakings decree an astonishing measure of courage.

Personally, I had to re-learn how to exert my independence and execute my choices in a healthy way, in an unbalanced world. Many professionals are not accustomed to a 'good mood' in the professional field, but ladies, the onus is upon us to command the tone and the narrative. It's an advantage for any association to have access to you, so in turn, model your brand as though it is a precious commodity.

I am a commercial healthcare executive, with 30 years of proven experience managing customer and clinician centric strategic initiatives within pharmaceutical, private and public health sectors in Australia, Asia, New Zealand, Singapore and Africa.

The arduous gradient of superficial interactions is enough to discourage the enthusiastic gift of the gab, shake up my integrity with effervescence, and hold up a mirror of my self- awareness, courage, and respect. I gleaned new dimensions of agility, flex, and influence in the thick of it. Once I learned how to authentically value myself, I engaged, reacted, and detached in an empowering manner.

In South Africa, I worked for the government as a key resource to improve population health. This included developing business cases, processing applications for funding, implementing campaigns, developing processes and policies to be proactive, reporting to all agencies, measuring outcomes, and enhancing the models based on lessons learned.

I was responsible for HIV awareness and patient care enhancements, family planning, geriatric clinics, tuberculosis awareness, baby wellness clinics and sexual health in schools. Even the most experienced cadre will find it a challenge to deliver on all these key objectives. I began my career in this vortex and even on the rare day that I wandered in the perimeter looking forlorn, I quickly bounced back to the purpose of making a difference each day, to every life that touched my remit.

The cosmopolitan melting pot made itself acutely present in a pristine and profound format in Aotearoa – New Zealand, where I executed a stint in community pharmacy, before deciding to pursue a career in the development of pharmacy software.

The world was my oyster and I decided to hop over the ditch to Australia. I was employed by one of the world software gorillas and implemented the online pharmaceutical benefits scheme for hospital pharmacies nationwide. This was a game changer in pharmacy, moving from the snail mail of submitting claims via a floppy disk to Medicare, to clicking a button and obtaining instant payment refunds. Every single time I walked through the door, I was welcomed with open arms and smiles and every pharmacy was excited about this conversion. This successful project catapulted my career to working with additional world gorillas in the software industry: I enhanced and implemented several Electronic Medical Record (EMR) systems, in both public and private health sectors. I designed and implemented the first Health Information Exchange solution in the Commonwealth of Australia for the federal government and I also implemented the first interoperability solution for the state government of Australia.

Despite my Australian successes, there was yet another country, whose brave optimism and relentless pursuit of a worthy goal, inspired me. Singapore, where everything is state-of-the-art and cutting edge. In 2012, I moved states from Queensland to New South Wales, to take up employment with another world gorilla software vendor based in Sydney. This renowned vendor won the proposal to implement clinical software at a new hospital in Singapore. A hospital that was the first of its kind in the world.

Boasting 220 beds, across four inpatient suites, the hospital also entailed 18 operating theatres, an interconnected Medical Centre, over 200 medical specialists, all interoperable, with a five-star hotel. International and local patients are discharged and opt to check into the state-of-the-art hotel to recover post-surgery. Should any complications arise, the hotel system has access to the patient's longitude medical record to trigger action in the patient journey. Equipped with smart systems, the hospital is also built to future-proof the medical landscape.

I was headhunted and employed to apply my skills to develop an enterprise architecture for a project within the animal health sector. I championed the merger of a prominent brand, the biggest pet industry gorilla in New Zealand. With the Australian brand in both their retail and clinical business, I took technical proficiency and analysis to the next level in the healthcare of pets.

After my salient event with the clinical system, I became the candidate to champion the retail and time management system. The kernel of a causal narrative in the pet industry rose to new heights with a comprehensive Request for Proposal (RFP). The icing on the cake was two impeccable recommendations to the board of directors for both a Point-of-Sale solution, plus a time and resource management system. However, I felt my vast array of skills and experience were underutilised in this industry, so I made the swift shift back to human health.

In 2021, during the peak of the pandemic and the outbreak of the Delta variant in New South Wales, I was summoned to scope, design, build and implement a solution to manage COVID-19. This was somewhat like building a plane in the air and I also had to work under lockdown conditions. Thousands of people died from COVID-19, without even knowing they had the virus, or before even receiving their results.

After the COVID-19 testing process, the system could not process the volume of work required to contact positive-testing patients in time to begin treatment. Local hospitals were at capacity. As a result, a local Health District reached out for assistance to manage the crisis. I collaborated with three private vendors to scope, design, build, test and implement a 'Call Centre Triage' process and a COVID-19 home monitoring app. The pathway for patients older than 60 years old was also to be managed at the hospitals.

It was my integral role to assess the bottleneck issues we were facing daily. One major issue was that patients who tested positive for COVID-19 could not be frequently contacted, due to incorrect contact phone numbers being recorded. Therefore, I reviewed and streamlined the process to enhance data collection. I also implemented a QR Code scan functionality and validated phone numbers before testing. Other local Health Districts reached out to implement the same solution and soon enough, positive feedback from many avenues gushed in, including the health minister.

This critical change to our pressured health system was mandatory, people were losing their lives as a result of gaps in the system. Change was the only constant. This was sink or swim. Life or death.

I showed up as a professional to make a material difference and foster positive change in our health system here in Australia. Today, the solution is recognised as digital health innovation by the Australian Digital Health Agency and was even exhibited at the 2022 Digital Health Festival in Melbourne, Australia.

Despite all the innovation, rest assured I faced relentless challenges as well. I have been bullied, discriminated, underpaid, overworked, silenced, made redundant, segregated, shut out of collaboration, victimised, had my hardware and office moved during sick leave with no communication, and the whole gamut. I was employed by entities that blasted company values in neon colours, but rarely lived by them.

When an effort was made to address misconduct, Human Resources was always on another page, listening to a manager and contriving outcomes. I quickly learned to never knock at that door again. I had a recruiting agent pinch a substantial amount of money from me and when I reported it to Fair Work and presented it to the table, he continued to bully me, saying I was above the award to seek a resolution from Fair Work. He then made a deal with Fair Work to release half of my money, provided I would not pursue the rest. Nothing is fair in love, war, or work.

One of my ex-managers once asked me to come and babysit his son over the weekend, while his parents were visiting from the United Kingdom. His babysitter had left him in the lurch, and he knew I was dependable. I dropped everything and showed up, after hours and with nothing to measure on the pay scale – just a 'pro bono uber eats dinner.'

Months later, this same manager stuck a dagger in my back and got me fired, so he could be the tall poppy on a particular project. The organisation rewarded him with a promotion, that was just how it rolled. Let's just say I have learned to train my heart to handle disillusionment, particularly from those I trusted. Put simply, a warrior of enthusiasm inspires both attitude and actions, and I had to dig deep to find my balance.

A brave woman is someone who is determined and indomitable in the face of preposterous battle. Calculated, bold women become unstoppable forces of innovation, vigour and influence that recuperate the lives of everyone around them. A brave woman is one who is not afraid to break the mould and challenge the status quo, in order to command, revolutionise and invent.

A valiant woman is one that is robust, one that springs back in the face of trials and gets back up, no matter how many times she is knocked down. A community of durable women are those that sustain and encourage each other, to generate a sisterhood that always has each other's back, no matter what happens.

Work life balance is most definitely not made of giggles, spirit sprinkles and ignorant bliss. Some days I had to tame a beast that was out of control, yet no one in the office got the memo that I was in a foreign country all by myself, no support network, living with excruciating pain – undiagnosed endometriosis, navigating through infertility, traversing through several bouts of failed IVF, dealing with several miscarriages, nursing divorce scars, betrayal from friends, living through domestic violence and being invisible in the massive crowd.

Each day I had to make a choice to get up out of bed with grit, align with positivity and focus on the action of the day. I had to seek joy with intent and relentlessly pursued continual improvement. I had to craft a heart ample enough to stock oodles of ache. I had to fathom how to summon therapeutic laughter, to reconcile my injuries. I had to unravel ferocious aspiration, to jolt sparks of innovation and creativity. The general cohort around me became intimidated by my confidence and ability to excel. It scared them because they didn't understand what fuelled me.

The pain of walking into the unfamiliar is the epitome for disaster, but I mastered the art of complex projects, in comparison to life, they seemed like a walk in the park. My finesse intrigued my colleagues. They viewed the exterior and appeared jealous, but very rarely took time to get to know the pain within. Alacrity was active and passionately alive in every organisation.

My presence was my weapon and I decided to change the narrative and step away from social suicide in the corporate wilderness. I treated people the way I preferred to be treated. The law of parsimony came to light in so many palpable ways, when takers just wanted to use my generosity and kind heart, despicable and cantankerous bouts of personalities came to the forefront.

We are all bombarded with the salient needs to be authentic and vulnerable, yet when we summon the courage to do so, it is often met with delight. Management and Human Resources prefer to not peel back the layers and deal with the root cause. Most frequently, the ostrich syndrome is thrust upon us, and we are mandated to develop amnesia and move on. Employment is also about the right fit within a culture where your values align. I will never sell my soul in exchange for a salary. I will always exert my freedom and execute my choices. I am the example by the command of my decision.

Some people refrain from helping or supporting you, as they are too agitated to sustain you in public, due to the contempt they hold of you in private. Understand the undercurrent at play and learn to protect yourself, as no one else will be capable of managing your shattered heart.

I am a powerhouse that leads by example, ensuring ethical processes. I have worked in a corporate environment for more than 30 years, and I have extensive knowledge and understanding of policies, legislation and core values impacting the health system and human performance.

As a company director and co-worker, I use the PLUS Model:

P = Policies and Procedures – I ensure my decisions, behaviour and deliverables align.
L = Legal – I portion my input to not violate any laws.
U = Universal – I measure my decision in line with the company's core values.
S = Self – I self-introspect to ascertain if it meets my standards of honesty and fairness.

Respecting yourself is about holding your own space and not compromising on your personal values, when the going gets tough. Respecting others means trusting their opinion and valuing them, even when you disagree with them. Hitting rock bottom, you will most definitely meet some dregs along the way. Be certain not to dwell in this terrain, merely treat it as a passing season and never unpack your bags or get comfortable. Implement a mindset alongside actions that will carry you to greener pastures.

Many organisations have cleverly established the inability to explain their conduct. Lack of accountability spreads like larvae from a volcano. Ultimately, we can all make a choice about how to show up in this equation – bitter and better. Even when mercurial gusts sweep the room with a distinct tone of supremacy, develop the art to trace the lay of the land with your vision focused on the future. Do not allow external peculiarities to derail you. Rather focus on a strategy to quell the truculence.

A warrior marches on, even in trepidation, I sanctioned the jagged power a seat at the table. I grasped the diplomacy to decency and appointed the habitation and purpose in my life. I welcomed them, listened with determination, then decided whether or not I had a purpose to remain. I also gleaned to never carry any guilt from letting others down.

The ultimate commitment is my welfare. I mastered the art to gauge a range of feedback from peers, managers, executives, stakeholders, external vendors, and mentors, discerning what to ignore. I had to proactively diffuse the culture of 'hushing up', to quash the stronger truths.

This was a strategic game changer to ensure none of us in the arena became inebriated on habits that permitted them to derail what was purposefully scoped. A complex working environment and an array of personalities creates a vortex for a day at the office. Granted that I do not wear my wounds on my sleeve, I had to teach myself to shelve my wounds from my personal life and perform at my ultimate best.

Even on days that my body was haemorrhaging my IVF pregnancy off like it was another assigned task, my colleagues and managers were more focused on deliverables, rather than empathy. I had to learn how to calm the internal storm and contend with the external turbulence simultaneously. I had to learn to focus on what mattered personally, then juggle the corporate ball, trying to find the perfect balance.

Every single day I leapt to the challenge to thrive, not merely survive. I projected a path to sharpen my instincts for professionalism. "The brave man is not he who does not feel afraid, but he who conquers that fear." – Nelson Mandela. Valour comes in numerous forms. Gallantry on the battlefield is just one facet. Frequently, it stems from the simple everyday decisions to try and fail, rather than failing to try. When negotiating, do not aim for the biggest piece of the pie, instead create a better pie altogether. Make a material difference when, and however, you can. Ruminate on the fact that at your funeral, no one will remember what you did, they will only remember how you made them feel.

> *"Waiting for circumstances to change so you can feel good is like looking in the mirror and waiting for your reflection to smile first." –*
> *Basher.*

It may be the zealot circus, but I had all the tricks up my sleeve. I understood my vision, I changed the narrative with accountability, I sprinkled integrity everywhere, I surfaced like a phoenix to meet every challenge in the eye of the storm, I discerned when to grovel for my humble pie, I broke away from the doormat mentality and became intrigued with speaking boldly and finally, I fundamentally gleaned the difference between right and wrong.

This is an authentic recipe for the ultimate 'Heart Warriors' – one who knows real combat and the taste of victory. I have never settled for the artificial light, and although the corporate jungle sometimes found me lost, I knew without a shadow of doubt that I deserved superiority, so I donned my warrior heart and carved it out to serve it up.

A healthy organisation will reward wholesome behaviours and eliminate a toxic culture. Many organisations turn a blind eye, leaving their employees to battle the field and wear the scars. Unresolved trauma can store itself and manifest in the workplace in various facets. My success was measured by others, however I continuously deliberated on my satisfaction. Acquiring knowledge and qualification is not the final deal. Instead, progress begins when we use our skills to develop and excel. Integrity is a two-way street, don't feel compelled to be loyal to an organisation that refuses to bring integrity out to play. Even if your heart pounds like thunder, find your warrior stability and relentless values to expand your true equilibrium.

Performance requires professionalism. I contributed professionally despite my broken emotions. What did your warrior heart defy? Bifurcation is the process of splitting something into two. For example, bifurcation allows one to get divorced, while leaving property issues to settle at a later date. When the day, project, team, manager, or the world, seem overwhelming, recall, and lean into the bifurcation process to deal only with what you have the energy for. The rest will find itself on your future agenda.

Take a page from this process and focus on the fundamental task at hand, while you manage the rest later. Remember, a Warrior is not crafted by default, but instead leads with their wholesome heart, which is grounded by their true character, not the pecking order of a profession.

THE COURAGE OF VULNERABILITY

DR LAURA COBB

Please note, this chapter contains references to childhood abuse. If this triggers anything within you, please seek professional help.

Mark Twain once wrote, "The two most important days of your life are the day you were born and the day you find out why." I've lived more 'why-days' than I can count. Each one involved a transformational connection with a person, piece of art, music, or nature. I've realised that there isn't a single 'why-day.' Instead, our purpose unfolds over a series of events, experienced throughout our lives by creating meaningful relationships.

Connection is undoubtedly our primary human need. To know that we matter and have made a difference in the world forces us to be seen. This risk involves a life of deep, intimate interactions, or one of lonely isolation. There is no greater threat to our self-worth than that of showing the world who we are and resisting retaliation, with criticism or invalidation.

This vulnerability, which some consider weakness, is the greatest measure of courage; it is a gamble of exposing ourselves and the uncertainty of how others might take advantage. At some point, if we want deep, meaningful, connections we must courageously suit up and show up in our lives, so we can then stand up and speak up and create intimate bonds with others.

Growing Up

I am the youngest of four children. The quintessential red-headed stepchild with glasses, braces, and freckles. I have two brothers, one was the life of the party and the other, who was awkward and socially inept. My sister was a pretty, uber popular cheerleader 'Prom Queen'.

Middle school days were filled with mean-spirited criticisms, incessant put-downs, and vicious name-calling. Despite my pleas for interference, my mother and stepfather made feeble attempts to reprimand my siblings for their hurtful words and explained that since they never actually witnessed any bullying, there wasn't much they could do. My parents never discovered or acknowledged that a close family friend had been sexually molesting me for years. The abuse stopped when I was nine, but the trauma has stayed with me ever since. Consequently, I felt rejected, useless, and desperately lonely, as no one heard or saw me at home.

However, they did at school. School served as a respite, where I craved connection with my classmates. I wanted to hear the stories of the other children, to know I wasn't alone, to be acknowledged and validated. The third grade resulted in failing ones ubject for three consecutive terms. My parents threatened consequences if I earned the same failing grade on my final report card. I did, but I resolved to stay after school to change the grade to a pass. Later that night, I lay awake in bed, content that my parents thought I was reformed.

A week later, I was heaving and sobbing on that same bed, burping up bubbles, my throat raw from throwing up the dishwashing liquid I had been forced to drink. My parents discovered what I had done through a friend. I was grounded in my bedroom until school began again. The bullying stopped, as my siblings were warned of consequences if they interacted with me. The molestation also stopped. Once again, I was silenced until school began in the fall.

Whilst alone in my room, my mind retreated to the same question I'd been asking myself for so long, "What is the matter with you?" No one, not even me, considered asking, "What happened to you?" Instead, I became an expert at healing others, taking great lengths to please people, to deflect any suspicion of my own self-loathing.

My parents remained focused on building their careers and bank accounts. The only reason I knew they were showing a sudden interest in my behaviour, was because they'd discovered and read my journal. My stepfather didn't speak to me for a year, as he couldn't cope with my promiscuity. This felt like an additional abandonment, one that kept my voice silent. My mother knew she couldn't prevent me from having sex, yet she had enough sense to have me placed on birth control pills to prevent pregnancy. At the same time, however, she refrained from discussing protection from sexually transmitted infections. We never spoke about it again.

All of this felt like yet another opportunity to silence me, avoiding important topics that needed to be discussed and refraining from communicating about emotionally challenging topics.

I always found it perplexing that my stepdad couldn't cope with a daughter who was discovering her sexuality yet was also trying to find herself. I was left to discover who I was away from home, with friends who were engaging in exactly the same behaviour I was judged for by my parents. It was obvious I didn't meet my parents' expectations, and instead was viewed as a disappointment, heightening my sense of not belonging.

I endured high school with the usual delinquent behaviour, drugs, alcohol, and sharp tongue. Yet, in my senior year, my parents tightened the reigns of my freedom. Before I knew it, my choices were limited, my curfew stricter and my privileges reduced. Realising and accepting their participation in my revolt against discipline, my parents relinquished their control over me when I left for college.

Armoring Up

I thrived at university. I quickly learned how to achieve and be accepted. Previously, my life had been under siege from my own, and other's unrealistic expectations, biased assumptions, and warped perceptions. The achievements I felt at university, however, first served to deflect the extreme self-loathing I felt about myself.

I became addicted to the overwhelming praise and adoration I received after earning every scholarship, award, and degree. My heart begged, "STOP! I need to be, not do!" Yet, I continued to feel as though I couldn't be me, because I didn't know who I was. I became a robot with a scorecard, an external validation junkie with an inferiority complex.

Twelve years after the first day of college, I walked across the graduation stage and looked over my shoulder as the dean said, "Congratulations Dr. Cobb." The name seemed foreign to me, as though it was meant for someone else. Realising she was talking to me, I continued to my seat, adrenaline pumping, heart racing. For a few seconds, I felt overwhelmed, yet knew I'd earned this title. I was finally the "Dr. Laura" my parents had always yearned for.

As I looked around at all the other newly appointed "doctors" I thought, "That's it? What just happened? Where are the balloons? The parade? I thought all my problems would fade upon being awarded this amazing achievement. Yet of course that didn't happen. Not even in my heart. In fact, that particular achievement was the catalyst for a 15-year pony show of setting the bar of success higher, each time culminating in a fleeting sense of satisfaction. If anything, my greatest achievements in life felt more like curses.

I constantly feared that I didn't live up to the title of "Doctor Laura" my parents had envisioned. My life was a relentless and exhausting effort to safeguard myself from criticism, scrutiny, and ridicule, by building an armoured shield around my heart, covered with badges patching over unseen, open wounds.

To ensure my heart was protected, I numbed all feelings of uselessness, with endless amounts of food chased down with alcohol. As the alcohol took over, additional consequences ensued. Eventually, I got sober, but the food obsession took over with vengeance. Throughout this journey, every minute, every moment, every breath was shared with Ana, my best friend of twenty years. Despite everything, she was always by my side and fulfilled every need, supporting me right up until I was five pounds from death, starving to be seen.

I craved connection, yet generated disconnection from everyone, including myself. Over time, wherever I went, whatever I did, there I was. I soon learned that if I wanted anything to change, I had to change everything.

Few people are willing to feel their own hurt, and instead take it out on other people. Those willing to own their stories are those who live their values and keep showing up. Yet, most of us go through our lives exhausted trying to be, do, and say what we think will meet others' expectations. Ultimately, we end up pleasing, perfecting and performing, based on something we haven't even confirmed with those people.

The thing that was hurting me, was me being me. I didn't know that I was the one inflicting trauma through self-sabotage. What was once a gift, the armour around my heart actually began hurting me, or at least prevented me from being the parent, the partner and professional that I wanted to be.

I didn't know how to be vulnerable, so I couldn't attempt having the courage to be in the wilderness and then become the wilderness. Standing alone is hard and terrifying, and we continuously doubt our ability to make our way through the uncertainty. This is the moment when you reach deep into your wild heart and call on your courage; when you move into it and stay with it. If you can do this, you will grow through the experience and make the connection with who you are, allowing you to live a more vulnerable, heart centred and authentic life.

Rising up

Basic physics dictates what goes up, must come down. Yet, like gymnasts, we must also learn to fall in a way that the injury doesn't prevent us from rising up and trying again. When it comes to living life, you need to decide whether courage is a value that is important to you. If it is, then what the critics and cynics say, doesn't matter. Get clear and name your values. Then ask, "What do I believe in?" Check that your intentions, thoughts and words align, then identify behaviours that demonstrate incongruency, when you've travelled of course.

Braving Trust (And Being the First to Trust)

Trust doesn't come before vulnerability. They go together. Trust is built through small moments of vulnerability in relationships developed over time, and from choosing courage over comfort. For anyone to trust me, I need to be vulnerable.

I'm not advocating for blind trust, which is a combination of a high tendency to trust, with limited consideration. It's smart trust, which requires good business judgement and good people judgement, combined to enhance your gut instinct and intuition, which is what I'm instigating for.

Next time you're called upon to lead courageously, remember to 'rumble with vulnerability' by showing up fully, living your values, being the first to trust and learning to rise above it all when things don't go according to plan. Courageous leaders are never silent about difficult challenges. Can you tell the truth, or do you give feedback even when it's hard to do so? Can you ask for feedback when it's awkward to have tough conversations? This does not mean being a completely open book and taking down walls. On the contrary, setting boundaries for yourself and your team can help establish the perfect environment for trust.

Being a trusting and trustworthy leader means being someone people can count on to do what you say you will do, including acting within your competencies and limitations. Own up to your mistakes and make amends. Accountability means that when there is a failure, you're willing to ask yourself, "What part did I play in this?"

There's probably nothing more vulnerable than standing alone in front of a group of people, whom you respect, that you work with, that you like, that you feel a sense of belonging with, and saying, "This is not the right thing to do."

There is honour in living in alignment with your morals, values, and ethics. What's necessary is the courage to believe in yourself and the potential in others. Akin to Glenda, the good witch of the North, in the The Wizard of Oz, see the power in yourself and tap into it. Then empower others to witness their own power and teach them to call upon their resources.

Speaking Up

I spent the first 30 years of my life disallowing myself to fit in. Whenever I've ever done something that's ever really made a difference, or contributed to someone else's life, I have felt alone and afraid of doing it. But at least I have felt alive doing it.

It is like being lost in the wilderness, yet, it is not about navigating the wilderness, it is about becoming the wilderness. It's about knowing you're going to be on your own a lot and that it's going to be okay. It's not about never finding joy again, but instead, it is about believing in yourself first.

Being enough

Confidence comes from living with courage. Leaders are not determined by their rank or status. A leader must be willing to be vulnerable. They live their values rather than professing them. Along with this, courageous leaders must (or soon will) know that if they are brave enough, often enough, they will fall. Each endeavour creates the opportunity to hone our power and tap deeper into ourselves - to harness the power we have within. When we do that, we own ourselves. No one can take us because we then own who we are.

Confidence develops because of our previous experience.

Confidence comes about because of your willingness to be vulnerable, to have the courage to show up and be seen, to ask for what you need, to talk about how you're feeling. Sometimes, our heart armour no longer serves us, it becomes too heavy and instead of protecting you, it actually keeps you from being seen and known by others.

Around 50, there is a developmental milestone when the universe comes down, puts her hands on your shoulders, pulls you close and whispers, "You're halfway to death. I'm not messing around. You have more days behind you than in front. What are you going to do about it?" It sets up a fork in the road, with only two options. We can either walk through the world in denial of our pain, offloading it onto others so we don't have to feel it. Or you can become curious about yourself and the world. That's the superpower regarding the second half of our lives. It keeps us learning, it keeps us asking questions and increases our self-awareness. I encourage you to always remain curious about yourself.

Don't walk through the world looking for evidence that you don't belong, because you will always find it. Don't walk through the world looking for evidence that you're not enough, because you'll always find it your worth and your belonging is non-negotiable with others. You need to carry the following inside your heart:

I know who I am.
I'm clear about that.
I'm not going to negotiate that with anyone.

If I fit in for you, I no longer belong to myself, and that is the ultimate betrayal.

Every time after that when I choose fitting in, over belonging to myself, it is excruciating. The most important aspect of courageous leadership is choosing how you respond to fear. Will you go autopilot and protect, control, or people-please and appease? Do you talk to yourself with shame and anger? Do you want to do this?

Within eight years, I got married, moved to Germany, completed a second master's degree, managed an overseas program for the education and prevention of family violence, presided over a national association supporting the education and careers of helping professionals, instructed university courses, successfully started a side hustle as a personal trainer and yoga instructor, and won local and regional fitness competitions.

My husband and I lived a frugal, childfree life for the first eight years we were married. He was a mid-career Army officer, and I was independently contracted by the Pentagon via the military. We generated a comfortable financial cushion.

The third time I fell pregnant and didn't start to accept I was going to miscarry the baby until I was about eight months along. I feared it being taken away, so I couldn't release my heart. I wanted to dress and rehearse the tragedy to beat vulnerability to the punch.

The problem with aiming to 'beat vulnerability to the punch' is, we tend to squander the joy that you need that builds a reservoir for when hard things happen.

Soon, my newborn son, newly retired husband and I moved back to the States and into my parent's basement. I was a scared, unemployed, new mother. I didn't experience the overwhelming joy I'd heard so many mothers describe. Earning a PhD in Child Development and Family Studies, teaching courses on marriage and family and ethics for counsellors and managing a program advocating for child welfare, did nothing to prepare me for being a mother. Within 24 hours of giving birth, I learned to change a nappy, breastfeed, and resigned from full and part-time employment, to care for this new person.

Gone was the external validation I used to define my 'armoured heart'. The patches deteriorated, as the external validation gluing them together disintegrated to expose the gaping, persistent, wounds. Soon, the addictions which once served to numb the anxiety accompanying my world accelerated, so much so that I contributed them to the divorce, instigated by my husband. So much so that I found myself homeless, without custody of my son. Gratefully, I spent only one winter on the Chicago streets, yet during this time also managed to find myself in two, consecutive narcissistic and abusive relationships. I found the resolve to free myself from that prison and now rest my head in my own dwelling with my special needs cat. It's a beautiful thing to wake up in the morning to declare, "Good morning God," rather than "Good God, morning."

We cannot always predict what happens after trauma, challenge and adversity. Our only hope is that if we do the work, plant the seeds, and find a sense of belonging, happiness will come. The path to business is not always a natural one. As an academic and U.S government employee, some parts of entrepreneurship didn't always come naturally to me, however, I do it anyway; I strive with the same courage I have always tapped into.

My final word is to be open to a different way, and perhaps see vulnerability as the best qualification there is.

REFLECTIONS OF A GYNAECOLOGIST

DR TALAT UPPAL

"My body is on fire. Call 000 please".

I collect patient quotes, with consent, to capture the powerful sentiment behind them. One day, I intend to publish the de-identified experiences (currently a piggy bank type arrangement with saved post it notes from numerous appointments).

Every week, I am plagued by the dilemma, why don't midlife women better care for themselves?

I am generalising, but why do women put themselves, including their health needs and wellbeing, last on their list of priorities?

My name is Dr Talat Uppal and I am an obstetrician and gynaecologist, based in the picturesque northern beaches of Sydney. My niche interest is caring for women with abnormal uterine bleeding. Many of them are also undergoing the joys of perimenopause. Of course, my lens is somewhat biased, as I am constantly referred to in quite severe cases, and my work week includes managing exhausted women with next to no iron stores, putting in hormonal based intrauterine devices to help traction the bleeding tsunami and sadly, diagnosing underlying malignancy in a few of them.

Why do women take so long to seek medical care for a fixable problem?

There seems to be an overwhelming tendency, by some of the clinicians or the women themselves, to accept debilitating symptoms related to menstrual cycles and transition of menopause.

The word menopause refers to the last or final menstrual period. The average age of menopause in Australia[1] is 51 years (normal range 45-55 years).

The perimenopause can start a decade prior and is characterised by hormonal fluctuations, onset of menstrual cycle irregularity and symptoms reflective of the lower estrogen levels in women's bodies during this time of life.

If someone is bleeding torrentially at 42 years of age, for example, and she is told that this will probably settle, it essentially means that she is being asked to 'put up with it' for a decade or so.

When a woman has had no periods for 12 consecutive months, she is postmenopausal. A fifth of women report no notable symptoms during this time, but another 20 percent are severely affected with nasty symptoms. In between these two extremes, are just over half of women, who report varying mild to moderate symptoms.

Common symptoms reported by peri- and postmenopausal women include hot flushes, night sweats, bodily aches and pains, insomnia, loss of libido, dry skin, vaginal dryness, painful sexual intercourse, hair thinning, urinary frequency, mood, and memory decline.

I am often asked about the need for blood tests, but these do not usually indicate menopausal status, as it is essentially more of a clinical

---

[1] https://www.menopause.org.au/hp/information-sheets/376-vulvovaginal-symptoms-after-menopause

diagnosis. In saying that, I am cautiously optimistic that in the future, the status quo will shift to one in which women are better believed, which is a minimum standard of healthcare that should be offered to all the community.

Midlife is also an ideal opportunity to review and reinforce good lifestyle habits including a balanced diet, regular exercise, cessation of smoking, minimising caffeine intake and alcohol, especially if identified as a trigger for hot flushes, and of course, explore strategies for stress management.

Menopausal symptoms are caused by lower levels of oestrogen that occur during and after this transition. The most effective treatment is Menopause Hormone Therapy (MHT), previously called Hormone Replacement Therapy (HRT).

Oestrogen tends to work wonders in this space. However, use of MHT needs to be individualised and only prescribed after an extensive discussion about the associated pros and cons, as it is not suitable for everyone.

For women with an intact uterus, progesterone also needs to be prescribed to protect the uterus from cancer (only giving oestrogen can increase the risk of this condition). Women who have had a hysterectomy are offered just oestrogen, hence, MHT is medication that may also contain oestrogen, progesterone and sometimes testosterone. It is available in different dosages and forms, for example, pills, patches, gels, vaginal creams, and intrauterine devices (IUDs).

I'd like to clarify that women who present with abnormal uterine bleeding must be thoroughly assessed to ensure that there is no underlying pre-cancer or malignancy brewing in the uterus including cervix, vagina, and vulva areas. Also, oestrogen is safest prescribed either through the skin, or if the symptoms are mainly vaginal dryness or urinary in nature, then can be given via vaginal route, using a pessary or a cream option.

Genitourinary Syndrome of Menopause' (GSM) can include other symptoms too, like painful sex due to increased friction, vaginal irritation, vulvovaginal itching, difficulty voiding, UTIs and increased urinary frequency.

Menopausal vasomotor symptoms, such as hot flushes and night sweats, tend to settle within a few years, however sadly, vaginal ones are typically longer lasting. After menopause, the vaginal pH changes to become less acidic over time, which also increases the chances of getting urinary tract infections.

Due to the declining oestrogen levels, the vaginal walls become thinner and less elastic. This can be a double-edged sword, with reduced vaginal secretions or lubrication, described by some as a 'sandpaper-like vulvovaginal'. The vulva also loses some of its fat composition, making the labia less prominent and exposing the clitoris in some women, increasing potential for chafing, as the tissues are sensitive and vulnerable. GSM affects up to half of post-menopausal women.

I recommend avoiding 'lycra' or nylon underwear and prefer women use loose, cotton ones to help minimise scratching. And wash with water only, avoiding the use of scented products. Either air or pat dry with a cotton towel afterwards.

It is helpful to try vaginal non-hormonal moisturisers to reduce dryness and lubricants, prior to sexual intercourse. This is an option for all women, but especially for those not keen to try hormone-based options, or if they have a personal or family history of certain cancers.

Vaginal oestrogen (cream or pessary) is helpful for GSM symptoms, as is systemic MHT, and will alleviate vulvo-vaginal symptoms for some women.

I am lucky to work in a multidisciplinary service set up for the wellbeing of women, and I honestly think it is a lost opportunity if women do not access a women's health physiotherapist review during this time, to get structured education around pelvic floor exercises.

There can be reduced integrity of pelvic floor muscles, resulting from a combination of ageing, prior childbirth-based injuries, and peri/post-menopausal status. Midlife is a good time to identify if there is any urinary incontinence and if so, put some brakes on. Life expectancy for Australian women is in the eighties and we can expect to spend at least a third of our life span in a post-menopausal state, so it's best to plan well.

What a multi-layered complex space this is. We are caring for a generation riddled with taboos around women's health conditions. Many have not had the opportunity to discuss openly with their mothers what they're currently going through. It is so pleasing to see the changing landscape, whereby, in the same practice, I am delighted to see so many mothers bringing their teenage daughters to a timely gynaecological consultation. The reasons for this could range from difficulty inserting a tampon, to painful periods.

Whatever the reason, the theme is the same, a generation of women aiming to do better for the next. This is a powerful cultural shift, a new mindset that will hopefully empower these women to be better informed of what is normal and what isn't, to have the confidence to continue to seek care when concerned, and not to allow anyone, clinician or otherwise, to trivialise their health journey.

Trivialising women's symptoms (deliberately or more commonly, unconsciously) refers to the act of downplaying, dismissing, or minimising the experiences of women when it comes to their health and well-being. This can occur when healthcare providers, friends, or family members, fail to take women's health issues seriously, or attribute them to other factors, such as stress, anxiety, or hormonal changes.

Unfortunately, trivialising women's symptoms can have serious consequences, as it can delay diagnosis and treatment, leading to adverse health outcomes. It may also contribute to the sadly, well-known systemic gender bias in healthcare, where women's health concerns are not given the same attention and priority as men.

Women need to be strong advocates for themselves when negotiating health systems. In saying that, I am cautiously optimistic that in the future, the current status quo, to one in which women are better believed, which is a minimum standard of healthcare that should be offered to all the community, will occur.

The patriarchy, or misogyny, of medicine refers to the ways in which the healthcare system and medical practices are influenced by gender bias, leading to poorer health outcomes for women.

I found the book, 'Invisible Women: Exposing Data Bias in a World Designed for Men' by Caroline Criado-Perez, really interesting. While not solely focused on healthcare, this book outlines how a lack of consideration for women's needs and experiences has led to gender bias in a wide range of fields, including medicine.

I also wanted to share that there is some evidence to suggest that female surgeons may have better outcomes for female patients. A Canadian study published in the British Medical Journal, a reputable health resource, in 2018 found that patients who underwent surgery with female surgeons had lower mortality rates and fewer complications, than those who were treated by male surgeons.

Other studies have found that patients treated by female surgeons may have better postoperative outcomes than those treated by male surgeons. Investigators analysed adverse postoperative outcomes for more than 1.3 million female and male patients in Canada, who underwent one of 21 common elective or emergency surgical procedures and the results were as follows.

Dr Angela Jerath, an associate professor and clinical epidemiologist at the University of Toronto in Canada and a co-author of the findings said that in their 1.3 million patient sample, involving nearly 3,000 surgeons, they found that female patients treated by male surgeons had 15 percent greater odds of worse outcomes than female patients treated by female surgeons.

While the differences in outcomes were relatively small, the findings highlight the importance of diversity in the medical profession and the potential benefits associated with more choice for the community of healthcare providers.

I would also like to raise awareness of the various management options that exist, for women who suffer with heavy menstrual bleeding. This is, indeed, a problem with many solutions.

Heavy menstrual bleeding (HMB) is defined as excessive menstrual blood loss that adversely interferes with the physical, emotional, social or material quality of life. It affects about 25 percent of women of reproductive age.

The Australian Commission on Safety and Quality in Health Care published national HMB standards, with an aim to streamline and improve women's health across the country, for this common and much under-recognised condition. The patient information 2sheet is a useful resource for women with HMB.

The 2022 Period Perspective' Survey by Bayer3, of Australian women aged 18-60 years old found that despite the high number (32 percent) of women who experience heavy bleeding, only 14 percent of the total surveyed had received a formal diagnosis of heavy menstrual bleeding from a healthcare professional.

Management of this condition (HMB) involves a plan to reduce or stop the bleeding, establish any underlying causes, and replace the low iron levels that women may be battling, in addition to all the other symptoms. Anaemia, or even isolated iron deficiency, can cause fatigue, which is the last thing anyone needs, especially the peri menopausal woman.

So, in conclusion, my two cents worth is:

Be an advocate for yourselves.
Midlife is a valuable time of our lifespan, and your quality of life is important.

---

[2] https://www.safetyandquality.gov.au/publications-and-resources/resource-library/heavy-menstrual-bleeding-clinical-care-standard-consumer-fact-sheet
[3] https://www.bayer.com.au/en/the-menstrual-load-1-in-3-australian-women-surveyed-believe-they-may-have-undiagnosed-heavy

MHT is a safe and effective treatment for the majority of peri- and post-menopausal women, it needs to be individualised after consideration of all pros and cons.

Abnormal uterine bleeding is important to investigate and ensure there is no underlying malignancy. There are a range of management options. Let us break the taboos around women's health issues and well-being together.

I must end with this incredible quote, "The management of my heavy bleeding and hot flushes has given me my life back, I love the new me".

WE CAN ALL BE A HEART WARRIOR

ANNIE GIBBINS

There are many times in your life where you will experience significant stress and a myriad of emotions. There are also going to be times in your life where you will discover true meaning, joy, love and hopefully, sprinkles of abundance.

However, because we know life to be messy, unpredictable and a continuous lesson in adversity and growth, we can't always guarantee how, or when, these emotions will take place.

I've always found it incredibly ironic that as humans, we crave change, but when faced with the very thing threatening this change, we tend to curl up into a ball and hide. Despite the best opportunities awaiting us on the horizon, taking the actual leap can be nothing short of terrifying and it is at this precise point that we have a choice to make.

Do we choose to embrace change, surrender to 'what if', or flee reality at a rapid pace. Although there is no 'right' way to live life, there is a 'right' way to respond to it, by tapping into your 'Heart Warrior' self, and professing to the universe, "I am ready for you, and all that you have in store for me".

Saying "Goodbye"

Throughout this book, you would have read the stories of others, who perhaps like you, have lost someone they loved, either unexpectedly or otherwise. Either way, both situations result in feelings of intense overwhelm whilst processing the stages of grief, shock, denial, anger, bargaining, depression, acceptance, and hope. None of these stages are linear, and typically, people experiencing grief tend to return to stages, bounce between them, or sit in some longer than others.

One of my favourite authors, Glennon Doyle, once quoted, "Grief is the receipt we wave in the air that says to the world: Look! Love was once mine. I love well. Here is my proof that I paid the price."

This happens to be one of my favourite quotes, because it explains that grief is proof of love. Grief represents the bond between the person passed and the person who has lost. The sheer complexity between grief and love is rife with opposition, however, in the end, pain values the love. Whilst this simple formula is layered with emotion, somewhere in there sits a Heart Warrior who will turn to hope.

As humans and Heart Warriors, we crave contact and support, turning to those we trust to help us navigate through the mazes of loss. If we try hard enough, we can reuse our pain for a greater purpose, digging deep within and finding the light and confidence in ourselves to push through pain. Although this doesn't diminish the grief, it does empower the healing process. Our wounds become our battlefield tactics in leading a life that we truly deserve. And you, my friend, deserve it all.

Can it really be over?

I don't for one second take my marriage for granted. When I met my husband, James, I was fresh out of school, new to adulthood and susceptible to falling madly in love. I am pleased to say, we are still madly in love. However, whilst I am a sucker for a fairy-tale, we have still faced our fair share of challenges. We raised two sets of twins, born just 26 months apart, and then welcomed our fifth child, into the Gibbins household.

It was, at times, extremely stressful. As a woman who has never wanted to compromise on having it all (*Yes, I believe we can have it all),* I always knew I wanted more. That's not to say being a mother isn't fulfilling, because it most definitely is and for many, I applaud those who devote their time to being a mother, because that's the greatest full-time job there is. But, as a child, I felt my abilities were never validated and my ambition to become a career-oriented CEO won over. The strain on the family was real, and sleep became nothing more than a short-lived luxury, between studying and night-time feeds.

However, not everyone has the perfect fairy tale ending. In fact, divorce and separation remains one of the most stressful life events that a person will face. According to the Australian Bureau of Statistics, there were 56,244 divorces granted in 2021. This staggering statistic is a stark reminder that many marriages end within nine years.

Overcoming a relationship breakdown can floor a person for months, even years. In recent years, divorce and separation has been stigmatised and suddenly, 'divorce' is seen as a dirty word. I am here to tell you that it is not. To love a person is not lost time. To raise a family and love children unconditionally, together, or apart, is hugely profound and important.

To desire happiness and independence, is the true spirit of any Heart Warrior. Perhaps, if you are reading this, you were faced with an abrupt ending; one you had no idea was coming. But I want you to know that whatever happens, you deserve a person who wants to jump over a fence to be with you, not sit on one wondering whether they can love you or not. Overcoming a breakup, especially when children are involved, takes a special type of bravery, one that is never a lost currency for any Heart Warrior.

Is it ever too late to start that dream job?

Erm, no. That is my very definitive and certain response to, "Is it ever too late to start that dream job?" Most, at least once in their lifetime, will face redundancy from a professional job role, or be faced with an unexpected choice to flee the boardroom. There is nothing more soul destroying than having your financial security blanket being swept beneath your unsuspecting feet.

Financial freedom is everything, but as we know, money is also emotional. The responsibilities, especially in today's economic climate, is concerning for most. With house prices on the rise, increasing unemployment across multiple sectors, no longer is a job for life. As creatures of habit, we can very quickly be accustomed to a job role, even if it doesn't light us from the inside.

Although it feels like there is nothing scarier than losing your job, I am going to flip that belief on its head and say that such an event can be a blessing in disguise. Have you ever sat in on a meeting on a Friday afternoon (What sadist holds meetings on a Friday afternoon?!), and thought to yourself, "What am I doing here?" I'm not demanding you immediately stand up and quit, or wait for a redundancy opening, because let's face it, we all have bills to pay. But I do want you to know that there is so much more out there for you.

When you ask yourself the questions that stir up professional doubt, I want you to explore your options. Chat to your partner about your feelings, upskill in your spare time, or take the redundancy pay packet and inject it into your dreams. This entire topic is so much more than a section in a book, but trust me, there is nothing scarier than regret.

Ouch, not again!

As an avid hiker, adrenaline junkie and overall sport enthusiast, I have had my fair share of injuries. Some would say it comes with the territory of physical pursuits, but there is nothing more disheartening than a body that doesn't work how you expect it to. Whilst I love hiking up a mountain, I do not like falling down one (take that as a metaphorical reference too). Sometimes, however, we don't always have a choice or heads-up that our bodies are going to break. Sadly, we have all probably been affected by an illness or injury that has floored us for days, weeks, or even months. With each ailment needing various recovery times, it's incredibly hard to stay upbeat when our 'temple' is being more of a 'hovel'.

An experienced yoga practitioner friend of mine once told me how she unexpectedly broke her ankle. Given her high profile job and the fact she was also taking seven yoga classes a week, she felt as though she was on fire. Her career was booming, her spirituality was soaring, and her body was stronger than ever. She felt at the top of her game, until a freak accident saw her in hospital with a snapped ankle. Overnight, she was unable to walk. I knew that her personality was going to be hugely challenged – one minute she was diving into the swell at North Bondi, the next, she was sweating up a set of stairs trying to use her new crutches. One minute she was living life at lightning speed, then next, she was bed bound for months.

Like many, I encouraged her to see this time as a gift of patience. Advice that did not go down well. Her pale, frail and defeated body was slowly taking hold of her mental health. She felt like a shell of a woman and the polar opposite of her former self. There is nothing more humbling in life than being taken back to basics – the need to enforce everything we have learnt about strength, the moment we feel anything but.

After watching countless YouTube videos on how to bear weight correctly, attending weekly physio appointments and finally seeing her bones begin to heal, my friend one day finally stood in the shower, completely unaided. Slowly but surely, she found her strength, and with much trepidation, sat back on her yoga mat for a gentle yoga class. Unfortunately, some poses are now forever out of the question and no longer can she wear heels higher than an inch, however, she is back to her old, positive, and healthy self.

The point of this story is that our bodies break and when they do, they will lead us on the path of recovery, healing both the bones and our minds. As a Heart Warrior, a few war wounds (or broken ankles) are merely battle wounds we learn from, demonstrating to others that we can and you can, overcome any adversity the Universe, or your body, throws at you.

So, what comes next?

I wanted to finish this anthology by acknowledging life in all its tapestries. We all have stories, fears, wins and so much more. There has been a misjudgement made about women, namely that our success has shelf-life. Of course, the idea of success represents something different to everyone and can encompass all facets of life, such as relationships, jobs, money, and health. In our modern-day world, it is incredibly easy to get lost in technology, social media, a traumatic past or any other obstacles that have hindered or healed us along the path of life.

As women, we are mothers, lovers, CEOs, healers, teachers, educators, leaders, creatives, innovators, change-makers, travellers and of course, Heart Warriors. Our courage is often involuntary, but courageous we are.

Throughout my life, I have met the most incredible women (and men), who have taught me what it means to inspire, empower, and mentor. I have spoken at conferences and in auditoriums, in front of thousands of people. I have led and been led to success. I have raised five beautiful children, and I know, being a mother is so much more than biology. Our ancestry is steeped in wisdom and experience.

My invitation to you is to never stop tapping into your Heart Warrior potential. The answers are within you. Your strength bursts from you. The love flows out of you.

The world needs us. Now. The world, that continues to shake, explode, and soar, needs you.

If someone were to ask me the exact definition of a Heart Warrior, I would say, "It's the person holding this book."

Never stop, never give up and never, ever, cease to be you.

With much love,

Annie xo

ABOUT THE AUTHORS

Annie Gibbins is a true Renaissance woman, with accomplishments in every facet of the business world. As an acclaimed TV and podcast host, keynote speaker, #1 best-selling author, publisher, and business mentor, Annie has established herself as a leading voice for women in business. Despite her numerous accomplishments, Annie's story is one of resilience and determination. She has successfully raised a family of five, including two sets of twins born only 26 months apart, all while building an incredible 7-figure business empire. Through Women's Biz Global, Annie has mentored countless women from around the world, helping them to achieve their goals and reach their full potential by calling out limiting beliefs, clarifying purpose, and developing strong business practices. Annie's story is a shining example of the incredible heights that can be achieved with hard work, dedication, and the right mindset. Her journey inspires women everywhere to break down barriers and achieve their wildest dreams.

Lumbie Mlambo is a Global Goals Ambassador, a UN Global Water Partnership partner and recognized as a UN Global Leader in clean water and sanitation. She is a graduate from Indiana University South Bend and Texas Woman's University. She was born in rural Zimbabwe, Africa, where she attended school until 6th grade and then moved to the inner city Bulawayo to continue her education in high school.

Inspired by her orphaned father who never went to school but served as a revered humanitarian in his local community, Lumbie took the leap to continue her father's legacy. As a result of her dedicated actions in serving the community, she started the 501(c)(3) nonprofit JB Dondolo, after her father's namesake. JB Dondolo's mission is to remove barriers of access to clean water, sanitation, and hygiene in underserved and impoverished communities to help reduce poverty and promote gender equity. Lumbie makes her voice heard about the issues impacting women and girls globally, sharing her insights and knowledge on how such issues can be addressed. She is passionate about improving people's lives and restoring dignity, which starts when women and girls have a seat at the table. In 2019, the United Nations Association of Dallas Chapter nominated and selected Lumbie for the UN Global Leadership Award for her work with JB Dondolo on Clean Water and Sanitation (SDG 6). She is a proud Tony Elumelu Entrepreneur Alumna and Ambassador. In 2022, she made Donors for Africa's Top 60

Women in Development, the Top 90 the Bayer Foundation Women Empowerment Award, Women In Management Africa (WIMA) SDG Champion Award, and University of Texas at Arlington (UTA) Community Hero Award.

Ally Hensley is an author, speaker, ghost-writer, content creator and stigma shaker of the best kind. Ally produces engaging, relatable, and insightful content for some of the world's biggest brands and emerging start-ups. Ally – as a creator of several global campaigns – understands how to reach big audiences with new ideas. As a versatile writer, Ally personalises her projects with authenticity and knowing that behind any brand is a backstory with limitless potential towards vision and sales. As a passionate storyteller, Ally is determined to make truth-telling through words, the next biggest trend. Dedicated as ever, since 2021, Ally has held the position of Board Trustee with MRKH Connect, Europe's go-to charity for MRKH support and awareness charity.

Karen McDermott is a multi-award-winning entrepreneur and author and the founder of Serenity Press, MMH Press, KMD Books, and Duchess Serenity Press. She is an award-winning entrepreneur, multi-genre author of over 40 books, Forbes influencer, 3x TEDx speaker, and a proud mum of 6. She's also an advanced Law of Attraction practitioner who teaches people how to attract anything they want into their lives and writes about her success principles as K P Weaver. Her annual retreats are sought-after events with featured famous guests and are hosted in an Irish castle. Her motto is: Where there is a will there is always a way. Her quote is: When time and circumstance align, magic happens. Karen is passionate about sharing her extensive knowledge and vibrant energy with others. She has a 'no excuse' policy: if she can do it, anyone can! Her vision for Serenity Press is to create beautiful books that live in the hearts of authors and their readers. KMD Books is there to share Thought Leadership, Self-Help, and High-level collaborations with the world. MMH Press is where she finds aspiring authors and poets and helps them to shine. In 2022 she set up Duchess Serenity Press alongside Sarah, Duchess of York to build out her series of children's books in The Kindness Collection and set up a YA collection that gives a voice to the issues teenagers face today. The Southport origin series has been picked up by production company CJZ to be made into a drama series that will be filmed in Tasmania. Karen has been awarded a number of awards, including the 2020 WA Ausmumpreneur of the Year award winner, the 2020 Women Will Change the World winner, the 2021 Think Network International Woman of Empowerment award winner, the 2022 Stevies Best Female Entrepreneur and the 2023 Momentum Visionary Leader of the Year. She believes in the power of mums in business leading the way for the next generation to live to their highest potential. Karen is on a mission to share the power of stories with the world.

Helen Glen is a Speaker, Author and Business and Mindset Coach, empowering women to go from stress to success. Helen immigrated to Australia from Bangalore, India at the age of twenty and by the age of thirty Helen created a multimillion-dollar empire from scratch, even before the internet age. Then came the recession, global economic crash, and divorce ending in partnership loss and bankruptcy. Helen found herself on "struggle street". She was penniless, homeless, and with three school-aged children, Helen had to fend for the family. Facing life as a sole parent was scary. She soon had some serious thinking to do, so Helen put on her entrepreneur hat and quickly opened a small country furniture store that provided enough for their day-to-day living. Life took a devastating turn when Helen's teenage son was tragically killed. Her personal loss left her shattered, in total disbelief and traumatised. Helen was resilient and had to overcome deep sadness. There were lonely, sleepless nights when parts of Helen knew she had to move on personally to make room for her "new normal" life. She spent many hours healing herself compassionately weeping and praying at her bedside altar, she used meditation and music to uplift her broken spirit. Helen knew she had to engage coaches and mentors to get her through dark and difficult times. Helen is a forgiving, kind and dedicated person of substance, who came out of retirement to study modalities of healing so she can contribute to helping women reclaim happiness, and loving living life authentically. Helen has a calming spirit, and her life experiences help her being a heartfelt warrior and just being inexcusably Helen!

Peiming "Sunny" Sun is the Founder and Executive Mentor, Sunny Life Solutions. Sunny has worked as a molecular biologist in Corporate America, but now is a Tiny Habits certified coach, an official Gene Keys Guide, a DTM (Distinguished Toastmaster), an Amazon international bestseller author, and a holistic lifestyle mentor. Sunny is dedicated to sharing modern science and ancient traditions with busy professionals over 40 who have loaded stress, self-doubt, and confusion. As a single mother and caregiver for more than 20 years, she experienced clinical depression, anxiety, and lots of self-doubt; as a result, Sunny started to have some physical & social problems, such as high blood pressure, weight gain, isolation and low self-esteem. After her spiritual shift in early 2020, she now calls these life experiences her "unseen grace" or life lessons with deep gratitude.

Sharon Lynne has had 40 years of experience in the industry as a Presenter, Producer, Trainer, Casting Director, Corporate coach, Entertainer, Singer, Actor, Dancer, and Choreographer. In Australia she is recognised as a highly skilled Broadcast trainer with an unusual and remarkable style of training that brings the best out of a person's delivery. She has acquired a reputation as one of the top broadcast trainers and casting directors in Australia, now also training and casting talent from New Zealand, the UK and Asia. For the past thirty years she has successfully trained and cast presenters for the Australian Broadcasting Industry and changed the lives of so many people by recognizing their true talent and preparing them for the TV Industry. In 2002, Sharon also devised the first inter-active casting website used exclusively to cast new TV Presenters in Australia. Born in South Africa in the 50's, Sharon Lynne has enjoyed a successful career presenting variety, music, kids and theatre critique programs. Her career started in the late sixties as a "triple threat" and over the years she gained extensive experience playing many of the sought after lead roles in major musicals including 'Evita' (Eva Peron), 'South Pacific' (Nellie Forbush), 'Kiss me Kate' (Bianca/Lois), 'Oklahoma' (Laurie), 'Guys and Dolls' (Sarah), The Sound of Music' (Maria),

'Grease' (Marty), and 'Nunsense' (Sister Robert-Anne). She has studied at the School of Musical Theatre in Montreal, the Actors and Directors Lab in New York, had 12 years intensive operatic training with well- known diva Norma Biagi and studied choreography at the Alwyn Ailey Institute and Martha Graham studios in NYC. Sharon is a qualified Drama and Dance teacher and for many years also produced and directed children's musicals and concerts for the South African and Australian public. "Second Time Around" is the name of her one woman show she performs in venues around Australia. Her 2nd passion is volunteering regularly at orangutan sanctuaries in Borneo run by the Bornean Orangutan Survival Foundation in Kalimantan Indonesia. She is an ardent supporter of the protection of this endangered species. Sharon lives on the outskirts of Sydney in the historic and breathtaking MacDonalds valley on the banks of the Macdonald/Hawksbury River, Australia.

Patricia Jo Grover, The Goal Achievement Strategist, incites action with the platform that she specifically created around her proprietary "Conquering Skills Education" to Encourage, Educate, and Empower individuals to achieve more success and be able to "Rise Above" any Challenges they may have in any of the 8 Dimensions of Life. She uses a heart – centred approach, that focuses on helping her clients have Mindset Shifts, create New Belief Windows, and find their Why and Purpose. Allowing them to Dream, Conquer Fears, and Create a Work/Life Balance so they can Have, Be, Do, and Earn more while they live their lives Purposefully, Joyfully, and Gratefully. her 30 years of Business In Management & Ownership, she has recruited, trained, coached, consulted, taught, and mentored over 3500 Entrepreneurs, Corporate Employees, and Staff of her own businesses. And is now working on her Ph. D in Entreprenology at the International University of Entreprenology.

Kelly Markey is a Woman Changing the World Award 2023 and the NOBEL prize nominee. Founder and CEO of Medical Solutions Pty LTD, digital and ethics advocacy, Kelly is a multi-time international bestselling author – across many genres: non-fiction, motivational, self-help, memoir, corporate informational, professional technical writer and journal. She is a well sprouted philanthropist, rotary board forum, toastmaster member, Jay Shetty coach blogger, writer for Women's Biz Magazine, leader, and supporter for creating sustainable families and educating children in Uganda. Markey has a strong partnership with Zululand Lifeline South Africa to improve holistic care, member of The Cancer Institute, Australia to support and champion research. Undergraduate of the human spirit and soul, fluent in five languages, vast overseas exposure and have travelled to more than 200 cities around the world. As an accomplished keynote speaker, Kelly is a strong advocate for equal opportunity and gender equality, Kelly has worked tirelessly to help countless of women realise their own strength and equip them to becoming economically independent, Podcast Guest, Brand Ambassador, YouTube Guest and in addition Kelly has graced magazines as cover features, radio stations, newspapers and television. Kelly is a novice poet. She is an accomplished woman, golfing enthusiast, and an avid reader. Kelly is an eternal optimist and trailblazer.

Dr Laura Cobb works at Union North America as a senior technical advisor on the Bloomberg Philanthropies' funded Data for Health Initiative. Her work focuses on improving the use of health data for public health decision-making in developing countries and the relationship between the food environment and obesity. Domestically, she has worked at the New York City Department of Health and Mental Hygiene, most recently as part of the Nutrition Strategy Program where she was the lead for sodium reduction in fast food restaurants as part of the National Salt Reduction Initiative. Internationally, she has worked at the US Centers for Disease Control in Hanoi, Vietnam, and as a Peace Corps Volunteer in Namibia.

Dr Talat Uppal is an Obstetrician & Gynaecologist who currently works both at the Northern Beaches and Hornsby Ku-ring-gai Hospitals as a Visiting Medical Officer. Dr Talat Uppal Clinical Senior Lecturer at Macquarie University. She has a DDU sonographic qualification obtained in 2010 which gives her an advantage of being formally trained in ultrasound. She is the Director of Women's Health Road, and has set up an innovative, digitally integrated, multidisciplinary obstetric and gynaecology service with in-house ultrasound facilities. Dr Talat Uppal is also a Clinical Senior lecturer in Obstetrics and Gynaecology at Northern Medical School, University of Sydney. Her past, decade long role was based at Manly and Mona Vale Hospitals, as Senior Obstetrics Staff Specialist and Clinical Director of Women's, Children & Family health. She is the past Chair of both the NSW State Reference Committee and NSW RANZCOG Education Subcommittee. Dr Talat Uppal is a Fellow of the Australian Association for Quality in Health Care as well as a Fellow of the Australasian College of Health Service Management. She is the joint coordinator of Diploma (DRANZCOG) OSCE examination as her special interest is supporting the role of General Practitioners in the Women's health context. She is enrolled in a University of Sydney PhD looking at collaborative models of maternity care. She is a RANZCOG media spokesperson and an active member of the RANZCOG Gender Equity and Diversity Working Committee. Dr Talat Uppal is fluent in 3 languages and has much overseas exposure with volunteer teaching work.

www.ingramcontent.com/pod-product-compliance
Lightning Source LLC
Chambersburg PA
CBHW030306100526
44590CB00012B/538